HACK YOUR
HABITS

9 STEPS TO FINALLY BREAK
BAD HABITS & START THRIVING

Joanna Jast

Copyright © 2016 Joanna Jast. All rights reserved.

No part of this publication may be reproduced, distributed, or transmitted in any form or by any means, including photocopying, recording, or other electronic or mechanical methods, without the prior written permission of the publisher, except in the case of brief quotations embodied in reviews and certain other non-commercial uses permitted by copyright law.

Disclaimer:

The information in this book is intended for educational and informational purposes only and should not be taken as expert instructions or commands. It should not be treated as advice or as a substitute for seeking help from an appropriately trained health professional or expert. While all attempts have been made to verify the information provided in this book at the time of writing, the author and publisher do not assume any responsibility for errors, omissions, or contrary interpretations of the subject matter herein. The author and publisher therefore disclaim any liability to any party for any loss, damage, or disruption caused by errors or omissions, whether such errors or omissions result from negligence, accident, or other cause. Adherence to all applicable laws and regulations, including international, national, federal, local, professional licensing, business practices, educational advertising and all other aspects of doing business under any jurisdiction is the sole responsibility of the purchaser or the reader.

Neither the author nor the publisher assumes any responsibility or liability whatsoever on behalf of the purchaser or reader of these materials.

The fact that an organisation or a website is referred to in this work as a citation or a potential source of further information does not mean the Author or the Publisher endorses the information the organisation or website may provide or recommendations it may make. Further, readers should be aware that Internet websites listed in this work may have changed or disappeared between when this work was written and when it is read.

Any perceived slight of any individual or organisation is purely unintentional. Names and characters of the persons presented in the book have been changed to protect their privacy.

The Author made every effort to accurately represent the strategies in this work, but examples used should not be interpreted as a promise or guarantee.

The examples within this book are not intended to represent or guarantee that everyone or anyone will achieve their desired results. Each individual's success will be determined by his or her circumstances, desire, dedication, effort and motivation.

Contents

Introduction		1
Part 1: Understand the Basics of Habit Formation		**9**
Chapter 1:	Why Focus on Habits?	11
Chapter 2:	How Habits Work	15
Chapter 3:	Why Motivation is Not the Answer to Successful Habit Building	21
Chapter 4:	Habits, Willpower, and Self-Control	27
Chapter 5:	The Secret Power of Systems on Autopilot	33
Part 2: Understand Your Habit Goal the 'Hack Your Habits' Way		**37**
Chapter 6:	The 'Hack Your Habits' Framework	39
Chapter 7:	Identify Your Habit Problem	41
Chapter 8:	Choose a Habit Goal to Work On	47
Chapter 9:	Set Your Habit-Based Goal	53
Part 3: Understand Yourself and Your Context to Achieve Your Habit Goal		**65**
Chapter 10:	Know Your Context	67
Chapter 11:	Know Yourself	77
Chapter 12:	Use Your Past Successes and Failures to Create Your Winning Strategy	89

Part 4: Design Your Habit System — 95

    Chapter 13: Pick a Cue — 97

    Chapter 14: Map out Your Routine — 105

    Chapter 15: Choose Your Reward — 111

    Chapter 16: Put Your Habit Loop and Habit Plan Together — 121

    Chapter 17: How to Break an Old Habit — 127

Part 5: Fail and Future-Proof Your System — 135

    Chapter 18: 5 Strategies to Help You Kick Temptations — 137

    Chapter 19: 5 Ways to Kill Resistance Upfront — 151

    Chapter 20: Guest Expert Chapter - Stephen Guise - Mini-Habits Strategy for Personal Development — 165

    Chapter 21: Test, Track, Tweak and Celebrate Your Progress — 175

Part 6: Tackle Common Barriers to Habit Formation — 185

    Chapter 22: 6 Steps to Discovering What Motivates You — 187

    Chapter 23: Dealing with Willpower Shortages and Outages — 199

    Chapter 24: Guest Expert Chapter – Martin Meadows – 5 Unusual but Effective Strategies to Build Lasting Willpower — 209

    Chapter 25: What to Do When Life Gets in the Way — 217

    Chapter 26: Help, My Support System Isn't Very Supportive — 225

    Chapter 27: 'What the Hell?' Effect, and Getting Back on Track — 229

Part 7: Bonus Tips and Tricks for Building Better Habits into Your Life   232

   Introduction to this Section: 234

   Chapter 28:   Focus on a Keystone Habit to Transform Your Life   235

   Chapter 29:   Guest Expert Chapter – Hal Elrod – How to Build a Miracle Morning Routine in 6 Minutes   241

   Chapter 30:   Guest Expert Chapter - Steve S.J. Scott - How to Stack Small Habits for a Powerful Impact   247

References and Further Reading

   Afterword - Where I Got My Ideas From   255

   References   258

   Are You Ready To Transform Your Life In The Next 30-Days?   270

   About Joanna Jast   272

   Also By Joanna Jast   274

In order to get the most out of Hack Your Habits, I've created a free workbook, which will guide you through the steps needed to create your own personalized Habit System.

Throughout this book, I will show you how to:

- Best design your habits so you start reaping the rewards from day 1.
- Keep going even when your motivation fails and you have no energy to carry on so you stay consistent.
- Minimise the impact of temptations so you never fail again.
- Create a personalised system that helps you achieve your habit goals and fits with your life at any stage.
- Create systems that help you achieve your self-development goals quickly and effortlessly.

Download your accompanying
FREE workbook today by going to
www.theshapeshiftersclub.com/workbook

Introduction

'First, think results. Then get them with the least energy.' (1)
~Richard Koch

Habits run our lives. Studies show that about 40% (2) of our day-to-day activities rely on repetitive, routine actions that don't require much thinking on our part. People who study success in personal or professional lives are aware of this - that's why habits and habit formation has become a rapidly growing industry.

Up until now, most strategies for habit formation relied on motivation and willpower. And while more and more people realise that motivation is not an effective strategy for long-term 'self-development projects,' such as building good habits, using willpower is the only other approach they know.

But in today's world (where we are surrounded by temptations) self-restraint and self-discipline have become even harder. Every hour of every day and night, we are bombarded by offers: cheap fast food, free samples of this and that, and no-questions-asked credit cards. Our world is the world of immediate gratification. So we fill our stomachs with food, our pockets with samples, and spend our plastic money on more and more stuff, knowing all along it's all bad for our health, wealth, and happiness.

HACK YOUR **HABITS**

In the new reality, overwhelmed by the need for instant gratification, our ability to resist temptation and willpower are no longer sufficient. We may have the desire and the drive to resist, but we don't have enough skills or strategies to do it effectively and consistently. (3)

I know how hard it is to resist temptations in the modern world. I have been there myself - tried and failed, for exactly the same reasons - poor willpower and a need for instant gratification. I'll share more of my story, and my journey to better habits, throughout the book. But as a trained psychiatrist and psychotherapist with nearly 20 years' experience of helping people change their behaviour and their lives, I also have a good understanding of human nature and the knowledge of what really works and what doesn't when it comes to behaviour change.

If you:

Have tried to develop better habits using motivation and willpower, and fallen on your face deeply disillusioned

- Are too busy with your jobs, kids, and bills to pay, and struggle to find the energy to carry on with strategies that just don't fit in with your life

Are tired of 'pump-yourself-up' methods and sick of 'inspirational fluff'

Dream of an easy, fast way to develop healthy habits that allow you to carry on with your life - without feeling exhausted at the end of the day -

then this book can change all that for you.

Hack Your Habits was written to help you resolve your habit-building struggles in a new way that's easy to implement. My approach to habit building uniquely combines a range of well-researched strategies and proven tricks. Contrary to common approaches, my system doesn't rely on having to constantly boost yourself with motivational techniques that just stop working after a while. My system is built on well-proven practical strategies, that once set up don't require constant 'motivation boosters' and can work even if you have poor willpower. Thanks to the Hack Your Habits strategy, you can develop a truly set-it-and-forget-it system that will help you achieve your goals faster, with less effort, and with immediate results - even if you have poor willpower.

As a result, you build a powerful, automated system that not only prepares you for modern day temptations, but also gives you strategies to deal with willpower battles and avoid motivational ups and downs. With that in place, you can carry on with your routines whatever the weather, your mood, or how busy you are throughout the day. My system has already transformed my life, and many other people's lives - making each of us become healthier, happier, and more productive.

I developed this system, because I used to struggle with good habits, too. I'm lazy by nature. I also have a sweet tooth and always had problems with weight. I used to hate sports and learnt to use food as a reward.

On top of that, over the years I developed problems with willpower and self-discipline. When I was growing up, we didn't have much. We lived in a small village, with limited access to the nearby town. Chocolate, exotic fruit, fancy, colourful clothes - they existed only in books and on the TV (which was black and white at the time). It all changed for me when I moved to go to university. Suddenly, those beautiful, colourful, tasty things were all around me. Even though I couldn't always afford it, I wanted to have it all and I wanted it now. That was how my problems with overindulgence started.

But, that's not all. My self-compassion, so important in helping me preserve a positive attitude to myself and the world, has a dark side: it lets me indulge myself in whatever I'm craving, 'Because I deserve it'.

Overweight, unhealthy, disorganised, untidy, doing my jobs last minute, with foul language and gossiping tendencies - that was me.

Of course, I wanted to improve. I tried the usual motivational techniques. I set ambitious goals. Put them up on posters. Visualised myself achieving them every day. I read tons of books and articles on diets and weight loss. I tried coaching, accountability contracts, rewards systems. It only lasted until the next 'Poor Me' or 'What-The-Hell' moment.

A few years ago, I realised I cannot rely on my self-discipline and willpower. Traditional approaches were just not for me, no matter how hard I tried, and no matter how motivated I felt. I had to find a better way of getting my habits and my life in order. I started searching and experimenting beyond the traditional ways of behavioural change.

I was surprised to find a wealth of evidence in support of a number of strategies that take human nature into consideration. Strategies that did not attempt to change the way people behave, or preach what would be better - but simply designed systems that outsmart our biggest vices, leading us where we want to go without judgement and all that 'inspirational fluff'. I tried those strategies and loved them. They helped me transform my health, wealth, productivity, and in general - my life. Now, I get up every morning to do my most important, intellectual work. I run and exercise regularly. I got out of debt and have some savings. I'm much more professional in my interactions with others, even under stress. I'm better organised, get stuff done on time, and follow through on my commitments. I've even managed to cut down on sweets and carb intake and - lost some weight! All that - without the excruciating willpower battles and constant motivational ups and downs. Now, I want to share it with you, to help you transform your habits and transform your life.

I developed my Hack Your Habits framework and strategy, because I know human nature - with all its virtues and vices, with all the tricks and games we play when faced with change. My simple, 9-step system bypasses motivational ups and downs, avoids willpower battles, and will get you to do what you need to do on autopilot.

If, like me, you are short on self-control, struggle with temptation, or constantly find yourself running out of motivation - traditional approaches to habit building will not help you much. Whether it's about sticking to a diet, exercising regularly, not shouting at your kids, or getting up early - you will continue to lapse into your old ways, struggle, and feel like a failure.

But don't despair. If you want to build better habits, break old ones, and transform your life - keep reading. Whether you are a complete habit-hacking beginner, or someone who has tried and failed many times, I will share strategies and tricks to boost your ability to develop whatever habits you desire and achieve a healthier, happier self.

In this book I will show you:

How to best design your habits so you start reaping the rewards from day 1

How to keep going even when your motivation fails and you have no energy to carry on so you stay consistent

How to minimise the impact of temptations so you never fail again

How to create a personalised system that helps you achieve your habit goals and fits with your life at any stage

How to create systems that help you achieve your self-development goals quickly and effortlessly

The accompanying FREE workbook, which you can

download at http://www.theshapeshiftersclub.com/workbook will guide you through the steps and help you create your own, personalised Habit System.

This book is organised in a logical, step-by-step way that allows you to develop your own personalised, fail-proof system. I have also invited a few habit experts whose advice I've found helpful on my journey, so you can hear it 'first hand'. Hal Elrod, Stephen Guise, Martin Meadows and Steve S.J. Scott will share their winning strategies with you, to help you implement those desired behaviour changes into your life.

This book is for people who:

Struggle with creating healthy/good habits

Have poor self-control/struggle with willpower/self-control issues

Try and fail to constantly 'motivate themselves'

Sounds like you? This book will show you how to tackle these problems and achieve your habit goals faster, with less effort and more enjoyment. You can just 'set-it-and-forget-it', and then enjoy your health, wealth, and happiness for the rest of your life.

Throughout the book I refer to the most common healthy/good habits: healthy eating, exercise routine, productivity, interpersonal skills, focus habits, etc. I do not touch on the topics of habits and addictions such as illicit drug use, smoking, alcohol/other substance abuse, gambling, pornography/sex, etc. If you suffer, or suspect you may suffer, from any of these issues - please seek appropriate medical/professional help.

Are you ready to transform your life with the least amount of energy possible? Don't wait any longer. Don't put it off till you feel motivated or are in a better mood. You've waited enough. The time to a healthier, happier, and better you is now.

Let's get started.

Part 1:

UNDERSTAND THE BASICS OF HABIT FORMATION

- Chapter 1: Why Focus on Habits
- Chapter 2: How Habits Work
- Chapter 3: Why Motivation Is Not the Answer to Successful Habit Building
- Chapter 4: Habits, Willpower, and Self-Control
- Chapter 5: The Secret Power of Systems on Autopilot

Chapter 1:
Why Focus on Habits?

But why bother with habits, you may ask? If nearly half of your daily decisions relied on a process, would you care to get the process right?

Habits run our lives. Studies show that about 40% (1, 2) of our day-to-day activities rely on repetitive, routine actions that don't require much thinking. 'Without habit loops, our brains would shut down, overwhelmed by minutiae of daily life,' writes Charles Duhigg, the author of *The Power of Habit* (3). All those things we barely register: getting up at the right time; turning on the coffee machine on our way to the bathroom (prepared the night before); our bathroom routine; breakfast; the journey to work and back; how we greet our colleagues, turn on computers – all that and more are automated behaviours we carry out without much decision-making investment.

Yes, our life is a sum of habits. But don't underestimate the importance and the impact of those daily routines just because there is little thinking required. A lot of things in our lives depend on our habits. Healthy teeth are the result of daily brushing, flossing, and regular check-ups. For a healthy heart, it's a healthy diet, exercise, and stress management. In order to earn your living, you need to get up in the morning, get to work on time, and perform your productivity routines. Good relationships rely on you being able to attend to them with day-to-day little things.

In a nutshell, your health, wealth, happiness, fitness, and success depend on your habits.

Moreover, habits can be built from scratch, replaced, tweaked, or dumped. Since science has deconstructed how habits work, with that knowledge available, you can shape your automated behaviours the way you want.

It means you are able not only *shape* your health, wealth, happiness, and success – it means you can accelerate it, too.

Just imagine, you get up in the morning, well before the hustle hour. You have time and headspace to meditate, exercise, have breakfast, and do your most intellectually challenging tasks before your family gets up. You go to work, get your stuff done on time, your desk is in perfect order – you don't need to spend hours looking for things, you're well prepared for meetings. Your mind is clear and sharp (it's all that meditation, exercise, healthy food, and quality sleep). You leave on time (since you've done everything and more), go to the gym on the way back. You can have dinner with your family or by yourself – healthy, good food (you remembered and had energy to prepare it). You have time and energy to talk to your family, friends, or read a book (since you've dumped watching stupid TV shows).

And all that just happens every day. No motivation struggles, no willpower battles – just automatically, day in, day out.

Wow. A fairytale?

Not really. It's possible. Maybe not all at once, and definitely not immediately, but with the help of daily habits, you can transform your life from being an unhealthy, unhappy, struggling-on-many-fronts couch potato, into a fit, healthy, happy, successful person.

Simply understanding how habits work can help you control them. Because good, healthy habits are built exactly the same way as bad habits. And if you can break them down to their core components you can fiddle with them and shape them to achieve the result you desire.

Lots of people have achieved that transformation, including me.

Now, it's your opportunity to transform yourself and your life – with the power of habits.

Let's look at how habits work, and how they can be created and changed.

HACK YOUR HABITS

CHAPTER 2:
How Habits Work

Now we know habits are crucial to achieving success in personal and professional life, let's look at how they work, and how they can be built and changed.

Is there a secret formula for creating and shaping our habits?

Yes, there is - it's called the Habit Loop.

The Habit Loop

The habit loop is a three-element self-perpetuating cycle that is behind any automatic behaviour (1).

The key elements of the habit loop are:

- Cue (also called Reminder or Trigger) - I feel sad
- Routine (also called Behaviour or Action) - I eat chocolate
- Reward - I feel happier again

The names don't really matter; what matters is how these elements work together. For consistency, I will be using these terms: Cue, Routine, and Reward.

Every habit rests on these three pillars: A Cue prompts you to carry out the Routine, which is then reinforced by the Reward. The more of those habit cycles you go through, the more often the behaviour gets reinforced, the stronger the habit is ingrained, and the stronger the neural pathway in your brain. If you're trying to change a habit - the harder it becomes to change.

1. Cue

Cue (Trigger/Reminder) - is the first element of the loop. This is what prompts or entices you to carry out the habitual behaviour. Cue can be a feeling or physical sensation, such as feeling hungry, or sad as shown in Figure 1. It can also be a sound (e.g. your phone beeping that you've received a new text message), a visual prompt (e.g. seeing your toothbrush when you walk into the bathroom in the morning).

Cues associated with rewards can create powerful cravings in our brains. Once this connection between the cue and the reward emerges, the behaviour becomes automatic - your brain will make you carry out the behaviour that brings the reward. That's why once your phone beeps, you can't stop thinking about checking the message that arrived. Or if you're sad and the *feeling sad -eat chocolate- feeling happier* loop is well ingrained in your brain, you will crave that bar of chocolate until you put it in your mouth.

One of my favourite examples of how cues work is my own journey to discovering the power of morning routines. Years ago, when I was in medical school, I tried to study while lying on the sofa or in bed. Sooner or later, inevitably I would fall asleep, no matter how much sleep or rest I'd had. This situation dramatically changed when I shifted from studying in bed/on the sofa to studying at my desk. I also went from staying up late to getting up earlier and doing my revisions in the morning. The effects were dramatic and happened overnight - no more falling asleep over the books. Now, with the knowledge of habits I've acquired over the years, I can see two different cues at work there: bed/sofa and desk. As most of us who are brought up in typical environment do, over the years I'd developed powerful connections: beds are for sleeping and sofas for relaxing, while desks are for working/studying. No wonder my body responded according to the cue given.

Since I shared my story and 'discovery' with other students struggling to stay awake during their study sessions, I've had a number of people write to me reporting that indeed, switching from trying to study in bed/on the sofa to sitting at a desk made a tremendous difference to their ability to focus and learn.

Cues are powerful tools for prompting our brains and bodies

what to do. As you can see, they can be changed and swapped to bring on a desired behaviour. Cues tell your brain it is about to receive something pleasurable, enjoyable - and it wants it really badly and wants it now. And your brain keeps pushing you until you satisfy the cravings.

These changes happen also at the chemical level, and traditionally, it's dopamine that has been assigned the role of the main driver of reward pursuits (2). Dopamine is regarded as the 'go-and-get-it' neurotransmitter (brain chemical) that pushes you to perform whatever is needed to get the reward. So if you find it hard resisting pleasure resulting from, say, eating chocolate or procrastinating by playing your favourite game, blame the dopamine.

Powerful habits can create addiction-like responses, where the person's brain in response to Cue will continue pushing them towards the behaviour until the craving is satisfied, even if achieving it is risky, difficult, and/or has a high price tag (money, loss of reputation, harm to self/others).

Sometimes, the habit loop becomes a powerful addiction loop. The cravings are so strong they have physical consequences, including shakes, sweating, headaches, and other unpleasant symptoms. If you experience any of those symptoms, seek professional help.

The key to mastering the Cue part of the habit loop is to understand what really drives it, what the craving is about. And it is about the third element of the habit loop - the Reward.

2. Reward

How do rewards work then?

Rewards work in two ways: either by releasing the sense of pleasure directly (intrinsic rewards), or through a learnt association (extrinsic rewards) (3).

In a simplified way, **extrinsic rewards** - those that we've learnt to associate with pleasure, are rewards that are external to us. Most commonly, these are money and anything that plays a similar role, such as material goods, gifts, praise, good grades, promotions, and avoidance of punishment, embarrassment, rejection, and any other unpleasant consequences. (4)

Intrinsic rewards are those that come from within us - things, activities, situations, experiences that we find inherently pleasurable. The exact nature of these would depend on your own values, talents, and interests.

The Anticipation of Reward

If the Reward is powerful enough to make you feel good after you've consumed it, your brain will make a mental note to come back for more. The more often you repeat the sequence with the reward at the end, the more the three-step habit loop is reinforced and the stronger the connections between the elements. At some point, your brain will start reacting with anticipation (and release the 'go-and-get-it' dopamine) to the Cue itself, whether we get the Reward at the end or not (5).

So this is how every habit works: you see/hear/feel/smell **the Cue**-> your brain releases dopamine, which pushes you to carry out **the Routine** that you know will (or is likely to) produce **the Reward**. We will explore this mechanism and put it into practice later in the book.

Habit Forming Takes Time

You may have heard that it takes 21 days to create a habit. Or you may have heard this is not correct. Indeed, the 21-day rumour is not quite accurate. The studies done to establish how long it takes to form a habit actually reported that the length of time it takes varies, and depends on the complexity of the habit and the person's circumstances as well as motivation (6).

On average it takes 66 days, but for some habits and some people it can be as little as a couple of weeks. For other, more complex habits and people with more challenging contexts, it can take as long as several months.

But don't despair. My system can significantly shorten the time it takes to develop a habit, so keep reading.

Next, we will look at the role of motivation in the development of habits, and why you shouldn't rely on it.

CHAPTER 3:
Why Motivation is Not the Answer to Successful Habit Building

I've got bad news for you - motivation is overrated.

But I also have good news for you - motivation is overrated. You can stop wasting time on 'motivating yourself.'

Don't get me wrong. Motivation is important to achieving any goal in life. Otherwise, you're just drifting without a purpose.

But there is much more to motivation than simply being motivated or not.

Let me start with the myth of needing to boost your motivation. If you're reading this book, you are probably seeking help with building better habits. Which means you realise you need help with habits. Which means you've done some research and thinking and came to this conclusion. Moreover, you've made that first step - you started reading and seeking better understanding on how to build habits.

That's a lot, isn't it?

So if you realise you have a self-development need, set yourself a self-development goal, and create a plan to achieve it, and start by deepening your knowledge on how to achieve it - to me, that means you are motivated to achieve your goal(s).

What happens next usually follows a well-known cycle of starting with the best of intentions and full of energy. Then, after a while (days, sometimes a couple of weeks; or as it happens with 66% of New Year's resolutions - (1) a month or less), you'll have a bad day, or your motivation will wane, and you're back in your old habit.

Here's the secret:

Motivation, by nature, is flimsy.

Studies showed (2) that motivation, by nature, fluctuates over time. Those fluctuations depend on multiple factors that are often difficult to pinpoint and keep changing. It may be your mood, it may depend on what you're doing, and it may follow a pattern.

If it sounds like a lot of uncertainties to you - I'm with you. This is why my approach to the whole motivation thing boils down to this: **motivation is a must-have when setting your goals, but it cannot be relied on to achieve them.**

The key to successfully using motivation to achieve your goals, is about

1. Understanding what motivates you
2. Ensuring your goals are aligned with your motivation
3. Using your motivation to build a system that will allow you to achieve your goals

If you understand well what makes you tick and set your goals to match your motivation, you're already winning by putting the right motivational fuel into your tank.

Putting the Right Motivational Fuel into Your Tank

As long as you have a good motivation, you're okay, right? If you want to start exercising to improve your health, or stop swearing for your children's sake - that's good motivation, isn't it?

Well, as long as your motivation is aligned with what you care about, then you're likely to succeed. If not - it will fizzle out sooner or later and you will end up not achieving your goals, however laudable those are. Just like Lilly, a client of mine.

> *Lily tried to lose weight for years.*
>
> *She wanted to be healthier. She had tons of diet books and wasted a lot of money on gym subscriptions, swimming lessons, coaching, fitness devices and apps.*
>
> *However she tried, it only worked for a while. Eventually, she started having health problems. But even that did not help shifting weight too much.*
>
> *It wasn't until she fell and broke her leg and ended up in a plaster cast for weeks that she realised how much her poor fitness was affecting her autonomy.*

> *In her head, her weight was not really a problem. Her poor health was a problem, but only when it started affecting her freedom of movement and her ability to control her life.*
>
> *So for her, it was not about being healthier, or slimmer, but about autonomy - the ability to direct her life.*

I've met many people who tried telling themselves they are motivated by things that didn't really matter to them.

I've been there, too.

For many years I tried to fool myself I was passionate about something. But what I really wanted was to keep getting better at stuff I found fun.

And I constantly needed new targets - because as soon as I achieved my goal, it was no longer fun. I kept looking for new things to do, and kept telling myself it was still in pursuit of that awesome purpose. My goodness, I did try to make it work for me. And because I can really talk myself into things, it did work. For years.

Until the carefully constructed structure started to crumble. I realised no matter how much I try to fool myself, to bend and stretch my motivation, it's not going to change. I am who I am.

With my integrity dented and my intrinsic needs severely starved of attention I was forced to stop and reassess the situation.

Trying to match my motivation to my goal cost me a burnout.

Now, after a period of nearly 2 years, I'm recovered and... still pursuing the same goal, but for a different reason. And I'm totally and brutally honest with myself. My motivation for pursuing this goal is what it is and I'm not ashamed of it.

I pursue mastery for the buzz the State of Flow gives me; for the surge of 'am I going to make it on time?' for the sense of personal pride from overcoming my weaknesses and outsmarting myself.

You can only fool yourself for so long. If it doesn't make you tick - it won't make you tick just because you want to make it work for you.

Whatever lights your fire, make sure your goals match your motivation, not the other way around.

Be honest with yourself. You don't need to disclose your motivation to anyone. As long as you don't harm yourself or anyone else - this matter is between you and - you.

Why am I harping on about it?

Because if you match your goal to your motivation, it not only means that you will be fuelling your journey with what really drives you in life, but also it means you will be setting yourself goals that take into consideration how much motivation you have.

If you only have enough motivation to run three times a

week, setting yourself a goal of running every day will be stretching your motivation beyond what you have.

Be realistic measuring how much motivation you have. The smaller the step you push yourself to take, the more likely you are to take it. If in doubt, underestimate - you will be surprised with the results.

And that's all that counts - starting yourself on the journey towards a better you.

See? With good understanding of your motivational drivers and smart matching between your motivation and your goals, you can avoid the big 'crash and burn' moments.

You don't really need to 'motivate yourself' constantly, or 'boost your motivation' when you slip backwards.

But don't discount motivation completely. Use it to create your goal-achievement plan and to build the system. I will show you how.

Next, we'll talk about another strategy traditionally used in habit formation - willpower. If you are like me, a creature of weak willpower, keep reading. I will share tips and tricks on overcoming your willpower problems.

CHAPTER 4:
Habits, Willpower, and Self-Control

So if it's not motivation, what should you rely on in your pursuit of self-improvement goals? Some self-development experts say you need to use your willpower.

Willpower, the ability to control your attention, emotions, and desires, is a vital ingredient of any recipe for success - in personal, as well as professional life. Without it, you will be constantly at the mercy of your impulses - eating doughnuts, watching Netflix, and playing Candy Crush - jeopardising your health, relationships, financial security, professional reputation, let alone your self-improvement goals.

I agree with the principle: willpower is more reliable than motivation, because even when you don't feel motivated, you can always force yourself to carry on. And many people are able to push themselves forward with the sheer strength of their willpower - muscling their way through it.

Unfortunately, as Kelly McGonigal, a health psychologist and the author of an excellent and popular book *The Willpower Instinct* (1), writes - many of the traditional approaches to using willpower are ineffective, or even backfire and lead to self-sabotage instead of help.

McGonigal's advice on improving willpower starts with a very simple step: understand why you fail at exerting self-control in the first place. It not only gives you a better understanding of how to create a support system, but also helps you predict when, where, and how you're likely to face a temptation hard to handle, so you can avoid those failures and prepare yourself for them better.

Moreover, willpower can be developed and strengthened - just like a muscle (2). The more we practice, the better we become at it. (Check chapters 23 & 24)

So, it sounds like willpower is a great strategy for helping yourself achieve your goals.

And it is. Except for when it isn't.

Willpower, although a good strategy for pursuing your goals, has its pitfalls.

Willpower Outages Happen

The most common problem is willpower or ego depletion. Research shows that we have a limited amount of willpower. It's like having a tank with a limited capacity. Just like with water tanks, every time you use some of that willpower from your tank, there is less left for later. The amount of willpower will not increase, until you are able to replenish it. (3)

Although new studies are emerging challenging this long-held belief about willpower depletion (6), personally I have experienced moments when my willpower is down and I'm aware of typical situations likely to cause it. That's why I believe understanding how you use willpower is important to your ability to develop better habits.

So let's now look at the situations that use up our willpower.

How Do You Use Willpower?

Anything that requires you to control your impulses, whether in relation to food, spending money, engaging in pleasurable activities, saying what you really think to that angry customer or your boss, or even having to stop yourself from freely expressing your emotions, takes willpower. So every time you exercise self-control, you use up some of your willpower.

Another process that requires willpower is making decisions. Why? Because decision-making is about careful consideration of various aspects of numerous choices. There is a lot of thinking and trade-offs involved. Most of the time, you can't have it all - you have to choose. And the more options you have to go through, the more trade-offs you need to balance, the harder your decision-making muscles work and the more willpower from your tank you use.

So the more extensive the decision, the more choices you have to consider, the bigger the impact of this process on your willpower reserve.

A famous study by R.F. Baumeister with freshly baked

cookies and radishes found that people who had to resist the temptation of freshly baked cookies had much less willpower left to solve some tricky puzzles afterwards, and gave up the task after half of the time of those who did not have to resist the cookies. (2, 3)

That's why it's so hard to resist that chocolate bar in the vending machine after a particularly difficult meeting, or a lengthy shopping trip. It takes self-discipline and willpower to do so.

Why Willpower and Self-Control May Not Be Enough

Over the centuries, strategies relying on self-discipline and willpower worked.

Unfortunately, in modern times, we face more temptations (4). With fast food, fast cash, and an abundance of products and services available at a click of a button, our self-discipline is constantly under fire. You may have decided to save for retirement, but right now you can have this awesome product for only so little and you can pay with credit card. You may have vowed to swap doughnuts for fruit, but even a short walk to your office is a constant battle with the smell of freshly baked cookies/doughnuts/insert your favourite snack.

We're not only constantly exposed to various temptations online and offline, but many of us are not equipped to deal with self-control issues. With credit cards widely available, money is often not perceived as a barrier. The 'you deserve it/you're worth it' motto is also often used as a way to push us to buy or do things that may not necessarily be good for us

Traditionally, self-control used to be taught at home, at school, or in church/religious environments. This is not happening as much as it used to, particularly in Western societies, and many people are left feeling inadequately equipped to deal with the temptations of the modern, consumerist world.

So if you're one of those people who do struggle with willpower and self-control, what can you do?

You can improve your self-control and strengthen your willpower (see chapters 23 & 24 for tips). You can also build reliable systems that will take your weaknesses and previous failures into consideration.

Yes, I believe that you can create systems that put your desired behaviour, whether it's healthy eating, regular exercise, stopping yourself from yelling at your kids, or avoiding gossip - anything you really strive to achieve - on autopilot in a way that does not rely on your feeling motivated and is not a drain on your willpower.

Doesn't that sound great?

In the next chapter I'll tell you more about my approach to building reliable systems on autopilot.

HACK YOUR HABITS

CHAPTER 5:
The Secret Power of Systems on Autopilot

Human memory is prone to error, distortions, and in general, failure to supply the right information at the right time.

That's why if you want something to work every time, you had better not rely on your memory. The best way to ensure the right thing happens at the right time is to build it into an autopilot system

Autopilot systems can have various forms - processes, algorithms, and standard operating procedures. They are created to not only achieve efficiency, quality of output, and uniformity of performance, but also - to make sure something is done every time it needs to be done.

Decision-support systems have been proven to be closely correlated with improvements in clinical practice (1) and clinician's performance (2). The importance of having good, reliable systems in place that eliminate/minimise human error, or minimise their effect on safety, has been well known in many industries, where safety is paramount - such as aviation (3).

Systems can guide your decision-making processes, or simply force you to take a predetermined option. For example, in machines used in anaesthesia, during surgical procedures, and patient monitoring, a pin safety system prevents attachment of the wrong cylinder to the wrong outlet and hence using the wrong gas - the parts just won't fit if you try to plug the wrong gas to the wrong point (4). A 'dead man's switch' in many machines and vehicles plays the same role (5) - if the operator is no longer in charge of the machine, the machine stops working.

Systems take into consideration the most common ways humans make mistakes and either eliminate or minimise the likelihood of this happening.

Systems can be designed so that you don't have to make any choices, not only limiting the impact on your willpower resources, but also eliminating any thinking from it. I run three times a week: Tuesdays, Thursdays, and Saturdays. So, if it's Saturday morning I know I'm going for a run. I don't have to check if I'm motivated, or worry about my willpower levels.

I've successfully built systems to:

- Get up early (5.15 a.m.- sometimes earlier if I have a Skype chat with anyone in another time zone, very rarely later)
- Exercise regularly
- Focus on the task at hand
- Take notes from books I read
- Capture my ideas
- Remember various little things without putting everything into my calendar

- I've also helped other people create systems for improving their focus, eliminating distractions and fighting procrastination, having a regular writing routine, etc.

This is why I believe creating systems that make you take a predetermined action can accelerate your journey towards your self-improvement goals, and towards better habits in particular.

My systems take into consideration my preferences, strengths, and weaknesses, my quirks; the limitations and current state of my context - internal (my physical, mental, and emotional factors), as well as my physical and social environment. I design them to guide, nudge, and even force me to take actions that progress me towards my goals.

I will show you how you can also build a reliable system that will run on autopilot and nudge you to take the desired action, whatever the weather, your motivation level, or mood of the day.

HACK YOUR HABITS

Part 2:

Understand Your Habit Goal the 'Hack Your Habits' Way

- Chapter 6: The 'Hack Your Habits' Framework
- Chapter 7: Identify Your Habit Problem
- Chapter 8: Choose a Habit Goal to Work On
- Chapter 9: Set Your Habit-Based Goal

HACK YOUR HABITS

Chapter 6:
The 'Hack Your Habits' Framework

My process of setting a habit system boils down to the 9 steps presented in the flowchart below. This is the framework I use throughout the book. It can be applied to any of the habit goals, whether you're working on developing a new, good habit, or trying to break an old one.

HACK YOUR **HABITS**

What's your habit problem?
(Your Habit Problem)

⬇

What do you want to achieve?
(Your Desired Outcome)

⬇

Is this realistic and achievable here and now? (Your Habit Goal)

YES ⬅ — ➡ **NO**

YES branch:
- Pick a Cue
- Map Out Your Routine
- Choose Your Reward
- Creat Your Habit Plan ➡ Future-and fail-proof your system ➡ Test, Track and Tweak your system

Middle:
Not quite/maybe/ to some extend

Go back to Your Desired Outcome and revisit the steps again.

Repeat until you have a clear **Yes** or **No**.

NO branch:
Defer and come back to it when your context changes

40

CHAPTER 7:
Identify Your Habit Problem

> *'If I were given one hour to save the planet, I would spend 59 minutes defining the problem and one minute solving it.'*
> ~ Albert Einstein

First, let's start with your problem.

So what's your habit problem? I mean, the real one.

Do you know?

I can totally agree with the Einstein quote above. The key to successful treatment in clinical practice is the correct diagnosis - the understanding of the problem.

That's why medical students and doctors in training spend so much time first learning about all the underlying anatomy, physiology, biochemistry, biophysics, and pathology; then mastering examination, interpretations of lab results, and x-rays, and all sorts of other additional tools before they are allowed to start treating sick people.

Yes, the price of getting it wrong can be very high in medicine, but don't underestimate the price of you misdiagnosing the problems you're trying to fix.

Jumping to solutions without properly understanding the problem has cost many individuals and organisations a lot of time and money wasted (1).

Addressing the symptoms rather than the underlying problem is one of the most common mistakes when trying to solve a problem.

Imagine you come to see your doctor because you have an irritating cough. You know you want the cough to go away. But if your doctor prescribed a cough mixture without actually exploring what's happening, your surface problem (cough) may go away, but the underlying issue will be still there, still unaddressed, and maybe even getting worse. Because a cough can be a symptom of various issues, most of them stemming from an underlying respiratory problem, but not all. It may be a side effect of a medication; it may be a symptom of an underlying heart disease, cancer, or even reflux. By prescribing a cough suppressant, the doctor may miss a serious problem. You may get rid of the cough or alleviate it but still have the problem, which will manifest itself sooner or later in another way.

And that's what happened with Ted.

Ted was a casual truck driver with an interest in software engineering. He wanted to do courses to gain qualifications in software engineering, but couldn't afford it, so he started freelancing, offering website setups and designs. He asked me for help with what he identified as a procrastination problem.

After I looked at his productivity system, it was clear Ted would often leave projects to the last minute, spend time browsing the net or playing his favourite games, and then rush to finish before the deadline. Usually, he would get it done on time, but it would not be done to spec, some features would be missing, or the quality was not to the customer's standards. Ted was worried about his reputation and hence further projects and money, so he started to look for better solutions.

He read time management articles and books and decided to use some of the most popular strategies. He tried Pomodoro techniques (working with a timer) and scheduling his jobs early with multiple reminders set up. He went as far as switching off his Internet connection to do at least the offline parts of his projects. But those approaches only worked for a couple of days, and then Ted was back into his old habits of procrastinating. He even came up with another way to procrastinate (he cleared his desk and did a lot of handyman jobs his mum had been asking him to do for ages).

Sadly, all of those strategies did not make much difference. Ted lost a customer who refused to pay for work delivered after the twice-extended deadline, and then another one who left scathing feedback on his page, following a job not done to spec. This was when Ted decided to seek help to 'get his procrastination sorted.'

Ted was adamant it was all because he liked the 'last minute adrenaline rush' and was a bit of an 'adrenaline junkie,' as it gave him motivation to complete the project on time. But just to make sure we had the problem 'nailed', we did the 5-whys exercise to explore if this was, indeed, a matter of his personal preferences.

Here is the transcript of the conversation:

Original problem statement: I like leaving things to the last moment because I like that 'adrenaline rush'.

Q: Why (1st) do you like to feel that 'adrenaline rush' when you're working on your customers' projects?
A: Because it makes it more interesting.

Q: Why (2nd) does it make it more interesting?
A: Because I like the adrenaline rush.

[Watch how this question circles back]

Q: Why (3rd) do you like the adrenaline rush?
A: Because it makes things more interesting.

[There is nothing new here, we're not learning more about the nature of his problem, so let's do a sideways step].

Q: Why (4th) do those projects need that adrenaline rush?
A: Because they're boring.

Q: Why (5th) do you find them boring?
A: Because they're too easy.

Here we've moved from a personal preference to lack of

> *interest/motivation for the task. These two problems, although resulting in the same symptom (procrastination) will require different approaches.*
>
> *Yes, in the short run the 'Band-Aid approach' may be to use an anti-procrastination tactic, such as Pomodoro, scheduling, or disconnecting the Internet. But, as it happened for Ted, the problem will resurface until the underlying, root cause is addressed.*
>
> *With Ted, once we identified the underlying cause of his procrastination, we were able to focus on solution-finding.*

Hopefully, I've convinced you to spend some time exploring your problem.

The key is to understand the underlying issue, and why this is a problem for you. Often people have a good idea what the nature of their difficulty is, but sometimes the true reason may be hidden.

Don't settle for the first explanation that springs to mind. Keep exploring until you get to the bottom of the problem. **The 5-Whys technique** (as shown in Ted's case study above) is a good approach, because the root cause is usually discovered by the 5th round; alternatively- stop when you start circling around. Just like we did with Ted, if you're not satisfied with the outcome, try going sideways with your Whys.

Time to take action:

HACK YOUR **HABITS**

You may have noticed, the Hack Your Habits *book has an accompanying workbook to help you achieve better habits faster. If you haven't done it yet, grab a copy of your* FREE *workbook at http://www.theshapeshiftersclub.com/workbook and use it alongside the book. This will help you achieve your goal of building better habits faster.*

Identify the habit you want to work on. It may be a completely new habit you want to build, or an old one you want to get rid of. It may also be something you already do but you want to improve. Once you've got it, ensure you're on the right track by going through 5-Whys exercise. Record the result in your Workbook.

Once you've got a clear understanding of your problem - move to the next step - **choosing the solution: the goal to pursue**. This is what we will discuss in the next chapter.

Chapter 8:
Choose a Habit Goal to Work On

> *'Goal-setting is powerful because it provides focus. It gives us the ability to hone in on the exact actions we need to perform to achieve everything we desire in life.'* ~ Jim Rohn

In this chapter, we will look at the process of choosing a habit goal to pursue.

This part of the habit-hacking process is crucial to success.

Your goals will obviously depend on what's important to you. But whatever you choose for your goal, I wanted to help make sure that you are pursuing a goal that's going to fix your problem.

A goal that really matters to you.

A goal that's achievable and realistic.

The key step of setting achievable goals that lead to a lasting behavioural change is to decide what you want to pursue at this moment in time. Not next week, not tomorrow, not when you have time, finish this project, lose weight, or get younger.

Here and now.

Once you've got a clear idea of your problem and the root cause, it's time to choose how you want to fix it. Below is a sequence of steps to choose an achievable and realistic habit goal to work towards.

1. Pick One Problem

Whatever it is, don't dilute your efforts. If you've identified a number of problems that need fixing, chose just one to start with.

Typically, I advise people to pick:

- **Frequently occurring** problems (e.g. you procrastinate very often, or you are often late for classes/work)
- **An issue with the biggest impact** on your personal life, relationships, career, etc. (e.g. you only procrastinate with a specific type of assignment, but these are major assignments, so not handing them in on time, or turning in low quality work has negatively affected your work performance, customer satisfaction, or grades. You may be late for work only a couple of times per month, but it's on days when you have an important meeting, and it may have a catastrophic impact on your career progress.)
- **Low-hanging fruit** - the easiest problem to fix - something petty but frequent or impactful enough to require a system to be set up to address it. It has to be something not fixable with one-off action, but requiring you to develop a new habit. For example, this would be not only about clearing your desk of clutter or introducing a filing system, but also keeping the

desk or the files organised. This is a good strategy if you feel overwhelmed with the amount or extent of work you would need to do to fix your problems. Getting something easy fixed first will quickly deliver results and is likely to boost your confidence to tackle more complex problems.

2. Define Your Desired Outcome

Let's start with defining your Desired Outcome.

Desired Outcome is a concept very popular in innovation and design fields, such as User Experience/User Interface (UX/UI), etc.

To put it simply, Desired Outcome is what you really want here and now.

Sounds obvious?

Yes, and no.

Many of you will be clear about the outcome you are seeking, like Lily, who I wrote about in Chapter 3. For Lily, it wasn't about losing weight or improving her fitness level, but about staying independent and in control of her life. This was her Desired Outcome.

You may want to develop a morning routine so you can get your daily dose of writing done before your family gets up. It is not really about the morning routine, but about getting your daily dose of writing done - and this is your Desired Outcome; a morning routine is just one way of achieving it.

HACK YOUR **HABITS**

In May 2016 I embarked on an experiment, which I called the Marshmallow Experiment (1) as a tribute to the original study on delayed gratification done by Stanford psychologists in the 1960s and '70s (2). The goal of my experiment was to refrain from eating any of the marshmallows until after a certain date. I came up with this idea because of health recommendations to limit my carbs and sweets intake to improve my energy levels, but the Desired Outcome of this exercise was not what was recommended to me.

I was not working towards eating less carbs and sweets, or losing weight, or improving my energy levels. My Desired Outcome was to see if I could exercise self-control in refraining from eating my favourite sweets.

Sometimes your Desired Outcome may differ from what you originally come up with as a problem to fix.

I love the idea of a Desired Outcome, because it really shows that often we follow goals we only think we care about (but really don't), or something we care about, but have no resources to pursue right now. Or we think we're working towards a goal, while we're actually trying to achieve a different outcome in this strange, roundabout way.

One of my most painful 'lightbulb moments' came from the realisation that the goal I was pursuing was really serving another purpose. For many years I worked more than one job because I needed money to continue with training and further progress in my career. I enjoyed all those side jobs, but they were also time- and energy-consuming. So, once I achieved my final qualifications as a specialist and got into a job that paid well, I was only too happy to dump all those side gigs.

Seven years, several new hobbies, a few more qualifications, and a burnout later, I realised that to enjoy my work I needed a variety of challenges; I thrived on learning constantly in an environment full of constraints. The Desired Outcome for my career was not, as I thought, getting to the top of my game and enjoying the benefits of it - but being constantly on a steep learning curve.

Whatever it is, don't just assume you know what you're looking for. Think carefully of the outcome you're expecting from fixing your problem; otherwise, you may find yourself investing a lot of time, energy, and money into achieving something you don't really want or care about.

The best way to start thinking about your habit goal is to start from the end result.

Think about the end result of the transformation you're seeking. If you're trying to fix a problem - how will your life look without the problem?

Describe your Desired Outcome in a practical way. No airy-fairy, 'I want to lose weight,' or 'stop yelling at my kids,' or 'double my productivity.'

Be as precise and detailed as you can, e.g.

'I want to reduce the number of distractions and limit my

procrastination so I can get my jobs done faster and have more time to enjoy my new hobby.'

or

'I want to stop reacting to my kids squabbling, remain calm, and let them sort out their arguments themselves.'

This is your Desired Outcome.

Time to Take Action

To establish a successful habit system, you need to be clear on what you want to achieve. Once you've identified your Desired Outcome, record it in the Workbook.

In the next chapters, we will look in more detail at the process of choosing the right Habit Goal to pursue.

CHAPTER 9:
Set Your Habit-Based Goal

In this chapter you'll set your Habit Goal. But don't write your SMART goal yet. I'll walk you through a few key steps in your habit goal-setting and show you how it differs from SMART strategy. Plus, we'll focus on two crucial ingredients of goal-setting that many people often skip or gloss over. This is a make-or-break aspect of habit goal-setting.

Why not SMART Goals for Habits?

SMART goal-setting strategy is very popular. Goals that are set as Specific, Measurable, Achievable, Realistic and Time-bound have been proven to be more likely to lead to success.

But wait, there is a little 'but.'

SMART goals are outcome-oriented: with a specific and measurable objective, that's achievable and realistic, with a deadline. So you know what you're working towards, what level of performance you're expecting to achieve, and by when. And this is great if you're aiming at, say, completing the first draft of your full-length novel by the end of this year.

But habits don't work like that. If you want to develop a daily writing habit, setting a SMART goal for that purpose (e.g., to develop a daily writing habit before the end of this month) is likely to cause you frustration.

Habits take time to develop. How much time they will take is individual, depending on the complexity of the habit, as well as the person's context - your motivation, your personality, supports, environment - everything we talked about in the previous chapter.

Which means: **there are too many uncertain variables to set a definite deadline for developing a habit.** And while you may be able to develop the daily writing habit before the self-imposed deadline, with so many factors at play, this may not be completely in your control. You'll end up not achieving your goal, and feeling like you've failed.

No, deadlines don't work well in habit development.

Another important aspect of habit creation is the fact that **automating a new routine requires you to successfully repeat certain behaviours time and time again.**

Often, progress in this context is difficult to track, particularly early on. It therefore requires a different approach than your regular outcome-oriented goals, such as organising your files, getting a gym subscription, or a healthy cooking cookbook.

In a nutshell: habit-based goals require a different setup.

1. Make Sure Your Habit Goal is Realistic and Achievable Here and Now

This is when we go back to SMART strategy and focus specifically on two elements of the acronym: Realistic and Achievable.

Why?

Because, lured by hyped-up 'reach for the stars' aspirational approaches, we love setting ourselves goals that not only stretch us, but also more often than we want to admit - are beyond our reach completely. And we end up not achieving them.

You want to go to the gym three times a week after work, but for the past several months you've been coming home after 8pm and hardly had energy and time to eat properly - do you really think it's possible 'if you put your mind to it'?

You want to get up at 5am to write for 30 minutes every morning, even though you have been 'an owl' all your life and your top-performance time is just before midnight- how productive do you think this is going to be?

Making sure your habit goals are realistic and achievable is the most important step on this journey. And this is where my strategy differs from traditional approaches. I am all about being realistic and pragmatic. All that inspirational stuff is great, and you should pursue your dreams. Don't get me wrong. I love stretching myself and I love self-development - I believe if you don't grow, you shrink and die on the inside. But you need to also be realistic.

So let's make sure the habit goal you want to pursue is realistic and achievable.

Grab Your Workbook and Look at Your Desired Outcome.

Go through the points listed below.

1. Do you have what it takes to achieve this goal HERE and NOW?

Once again, you need to be honest with yourself. Of course you can be as aspirational as you want, but being realistic will make you much more likely to achieve this goal.

Before you commit to any goal, you should ask yourself the questions listed below. Answer them as honestly as you can.

- Can I afford to pursue this goal right now?
- Do I have what it takes to achieve it right now? (motivation, skills/abilities, personality traits)?
- Do I have the time, energy, and emotional support needed right now?
- Can I afford it financially?
- How much adjustment would it take to pursue it?
- How much time and energy would it take for me to put those adjustments in place?
- Can I afford to spend the required time and energy on that?

Only go for it if all your answers are a clear 'yes.' If most of your answers are 'no', you'd probably be better off not pursuing this goal at this moment. Otherwise, you'll just waste time and energy on trying to achieve something you don't have the time, energy, support, or other resources to achieve. My suggestion is you defer it until your situation changes (more about it in the next section - Understand Yourself and Your Context). Make a note (put a reminder in your calendar) to look at this again in the future and go through this exercise again.

However, if you've answered any of those questions with 'not quite,' or 'to some extent,' or 'maybe,' you can negotiate with yourself further, e.g.

- If you don't have enough time/energy/money, ask yourself if you can free it up and allocate it to this goal
- If you don't have enough emotional support (e.g. your family doesn't like the idea of you taking up regular exercise), consider carefully if you can live with the lack of support at home and find support elsewhere (you can check Chapter 26 for tips).
- If you see that making adjustments in your current situation requires a lot of investment and you may not be able to free up enough resources to facilitate that, consider reviewing or adjusting your goal. The next point (What's realistic here and now) takes you through the necessary steps.

2. What's realistic here and now?

If any of your answers were not a full yes, consider adjusting your goal by going through the following steps:

- What can I afford to change now, given the time, energy, money, support, etc. available to me?
- How much or how little can I *easily* change within my current situation?

It pays to be honest and realistic with yourself. Yes, it would be great if you could just stop shouting at your kids completely, but is it really realistic? Maybe it is about just being able to remain calm when you tell them off, or not reacting to them when they're arguing between themselves?

3. Make sure your Habit Goal is appropriate and acceptable in your current context

The next step to ensure your Habit Goal is within your reach is to consider the wider impact of the changes you're seeking.

Humans, being social animals, rarely operate in a vacuum. Any decision to change behaviour, particularly if related to habits, can and will affect your immediate environment: your family, your work colleagues, office mates, friends, whoever else interacts with you in the context of the behaviour you're attempting to change.

Your kids may be delighted you stopped meddling in their arguments, but they may also feel ignored and definitely uneasy about the lack of familiar responses from you. This may alarm your spouse/partner. Being able to remain calm in stressful situations at home may have an impact on the way you interact with your customers at work, etc.

On the other hand, if you're starting to exercise and using the time you used to spend chatting with your friends for that, your friends may feel abandoned and ignored and may insist on you changing your new exercise routine. And if you get up earlier to go to the gym, this will have an impact on your energy levels throughout the day and you may hit a 'trough' at the time of important meetings.

In the excitement of 'the new beginning,' we tend to forget that changes we make will affect our environment. And the environment, particularly your social network, may push back.

In order to successfully achieve a behavioural change, such as developing a new habit or breaking an old one, you also need to understand how your transformation will impact your context, and specifically your:

- Social
- Physical
- Internal (your physical, emotional, and mental) environments. My approach to exploring these factors is to look at each aspect of your environment, as broken down above, from the point of view of its:
- **Limitations** (what's possible)
- **Constraints** (what's appropriate)
- **Props/Supports** (people, things, behaviours, etc. that can support or assist you in achieving your goals)

We will look at these aspects of successful habit system formation in Part 3.

4. Do you accept this as the goal to pursue?

Having gone through the explorations described above, you should have a clearer idea of what's possible/doable **here and now**, and what's appropriate/acceptable from various points of view. Ask yourself:

- Do you accept it as your goal to pursue?

And if the answer is no/not quite/maybe, consider the following:

- What's the nearest best/acceptable option?

Rinse and repeat until you have a realistic and achievable goal with good return on investment (ROI) and you accept it as your Habit Goal to pursue.

Pursuing habit goals that are not 100% acceptable or realistic

If you decide to pursue a goal that isn't fully acceptable or 100% realistic, always think about the cost (time, effort, money, emotional cost) required to overcome/change/bypass the barrier.

If at any point in this exercise you realise that the limitations/constraints you uncovered affect the ROI from the change you're seeking so much you are no longer keen on pursuing the goal, **review the goal,** go back to **explore Desired Outcome again,** or even - **relook at your Habit problem.**

2. Think Schedule, not Deadline

Unlike outcome-oriented goals - which are focused on achieving a specific outcome before a deadline - habit-based goals aim at creating a system, which doesn't work so well if you have a deadline for them.

Why?

For example, if you want to keep your desk organised (so not just one-off clearing), you need to build a habit around it.

Creating a habit of putting your work stuff away, keeping your files organised and drawers clutter-free will take some time, and requires certain actions to be taken regularly, such as daily after you've finished working, once a week etc. For these sorts of actions, it's better to create a schedule for your 'keeping my desk organised' activities.

Setting up habits is more complex than achieving outcome-oriented goals. Often, habits will consist of multiple actions that need to be performed regularly in order for the system to work. For instance, to keep your desk organised you may need to:

- Have a daily routine to put away tools and outputs or prepare your desk/workstation for the next day at the end of your workday
- Have a habit of keeping your tools always in the same place
- Have a system to keep on top of your to-dos
- Have a filing system
- Have a regular review/clearing schedule

That's much more complex than simply clearing your desk,

drawers, and files of clutter and organising them.

So for your 'keep my desk organised' habit, you may want to choose to build:

- A daily routine of clearing your desk of stuff you've finished dealing with and preparing all you need for tomorrow - and schedule it every day just before you're due to finish for the day
- A weekly review of to-dos (scheduled every Monday morning)
- A monthly 'clearing clutter' session - done on the 1st working day of the month

3. Focus on Practice, not Performance

Here is another difference between outcome-oriented goals and habit-based goals: habits are about doing the thing you're supposed to do every time you're supposed to do it. Because habits only work if they run on autopilot, getting to the point when the behaviour is automatic requires focus on the practice - 'showing up' and doing it, repeatedly performing the desired behaviour.

This is particularly hard early on when the behaviour is not automatic. That's why focusing on performance (how well you do it) may be more of a distraction, or even hinder the process completely.

For example, when you're working towards something with a specific outcome, for instance, getting your book finished in 30 days, you know how much you need to do to achieve it. So you may want to set specific targets, e.g. to write a chapter per day, or to finish the first draft by next week, second by the week after, etc. These are performance-specific goals.

But if you wanted to get into a habit of writing regularly, you would need to choose a goal like writing every day for 30 minutes. Add the time and you have a schedule - to write for 30 minutes every morning. Having a regular writing slot will likely lead to you improving your overall writing performance, but your goal here is not a specific writing performance, but an ability to write every day - that's a habit-focused goal.

So if you're aiming at creating a new habit, instead of striving to achieve a certain level of performance, such as words or chapters written, focus on practicing the desired behaviour every time you're supposed to do it.

Time to Take Action

Go through the steps described in this chapter. You can record the results of your reflections in the Workbook as your Habit Goal, but don't settle for it yet. To create a Habit Goal that is truly achievable and realistic, you need more knowledge - of your context and yourself. We will look at it in the next part.

HACK YOUR **HABITS**

Part 3:

Understand Yourself and Your Context to Achieve Your Habit Goal

- Chapter 10: Know Your Context
- Chapter 11: Know Yourself
- Chapter 12: Use Your Past Successes and Failures to Create Your Winning Strategy

Introduction to Part 3

In this section we will focus on making sure the Habit Goal you choose to pursue is realistic and achievable. These two aspects of goal-setting are often glossed over or simply ignored.

It may sound obvious, but people often decide to pursue goals they care about, but at the wrong time, in the wrong environment, or without the right emotional support. Some of us choose to work towards goals we may not care enough about because these are other people's goals - our parents', spouse's, or society's expectations.

Being honest with yourself is key to defining the goal you want to pursue at this moment. Not next week, not when you finish this project/lose weight/move houses - **here and now.**

CHAPTER 10:
Know Your Context

We'll start our exploration of how achievable and realistic your habit change pursuits are with a look at your context - the reality in which you live and operate - from your physical environment to your internal environment (your body, mind, and emotional world), as well as your social context.

Why?

Have you ever failed or struggled to achieve a goal because your environment got in the way? You had plenty of motivation, but the timing was wrong, or your nearest and dearest didn't support your efforts, or you were doing really well until you got sick?

I've been there too. My exercise routine for years relied on pool or gym opening hours, and my ability to get through the traffic to get there on time. No matter how hard I tried, I'd miss my session at least once every couple of weeks.

I've heard many stories about dieting struggles because of the unhealthy food lying around the house.

Sadly, when setting goals, particularly habit-building goals, people often ignore their context. They think the sheer power of their motivation will just carry them through those long days before the new routine is embedded in their lives.

Wrong. Very wrong.

Your context is very important for habit creation (1), because this is where we find our cues. Our environment can enable the routine or make it more difficult.

Context also means people around us - people who can support our actions, disrupt them, discourage us, or even actively prevent us from carrying out the new behaviour.

Your context, if not aligned with your habit, can jeopardise your new routine pretty quickly. But if you're able to get your environment to support your new routine, it will speed up the development of your new habit.

I've experienced it myself when, after years of trying to fit in my exercise routine around various requirements for my favourite sport (swimming), I switched to running (even though I never really liked it), making sure it fit into my context at the time. Once I achieved it, even though I still don't like running, I've been doing it regularly 3 times a week for over a year now.

Let's look at your context now and how you can use it to your advantage.

How to Use Your Context to Build Good Habits

For the purpose of this book, **the context is your**:

- **External environment.** It's usually physical space (your house, neighbourhood, workspace, etc.), but also everything else external to you, material or otherwise not human that has influence over your life (your financial situation, the weather/climate you live in, the laws of physics, and the country you live in, etc.)

- **Internal environment** (your body, mind, emotion, and spirituality)
- **Social environment** (people around you: family, friends, work colleagues, community, society, etc.)

My approach to the use of context/environment in habit formation is inspired by user interface/user experience approaches to building products and services (2, 3).

When considering how any of the three elements of your context affects or can affect your new habit, look at potential **limitations, constraints, and props/supports** this particular element brings into play.

This exercise can get quite detailed. I recommend that you write your findings down and organise them into a table. For your convenience I've created a worksheet where you can enter your observations. You can find it in the workbook at www.theshapeshiftersclub.com/workbook

This way, each aspect of your context has its own:

- **Limitations** (what's possible)
- **Constraints** (what's appropriate)

- **Props/Supports** (people, things, behaviours etc. that can support or assist you in achieving your goals).

In the next section, I'll walk you through the above mentioned 3 aspects of your context, and show you how you can use them to your advantage in building new or breaking old habits.

1. Your External Environment

Your physical environment is the physical space where you perform your habitual activities, as well as your time and financial situation.

For your productivity routine, this will likely be your office (work or home), your study room, meeting/board rooms, etc. It is also your desk or other workspace, your filing cabinet/system, your computer (hardware and software), and any other work tools.

For your exercise regime, this will be the space where you exercise, your workout clothes and shoes, any other equipment you need, gym membership or opening hours, etc.

When changing to a healthy eating habit, you will also need to consider all the places you usually eat (e.g. eating out, snack machines), shop, your kitchen - including storage solutions, cooking utensils, and recipe books.

When considering your external environment, think of existing limitations, constraints and props/supports that you typically encounter or may encounter when you're performing your desired behaviour.

For your productivity routine, limitations may be: a slow

computer, a small desk, or a shared office. The fact that you share an office and a filing cabinet may also impose some constraints on you, too. Your well-organised boss may be your support, and a company-wide well-labelled filing system may be your prop.

Once you've got the limitations and constraints, consider if all of them are real, or maybe some are in your head? Also think about the impact of the limitations/constraints on your ability to build or break the specific habit you're seeking. Are you able to overcome any of these?

Do the same for props/supports.

2. Your Internal Environment

Your internal environment can be further divided into your:

- Body
- Mind
- Emotions
- Spirituality

All four aspects of your internal world are important to your functioning. However, the most pertinent are the first three. They are most likely to interfere with your day-to-day behaviours and be affected by, as well as influence, your habits.

We will not touch on the spirituality aspect of self-improvement through better habits. Spirituality affects you at a deeper, much more fundamental level. I assume that if you're seeking self-improvement through building better habits, you have made that decision in line with your values, your inner sense of purpose, or any Higher Being you may believe in. If you haven't done that, or are not sure if this is the case, please pause and explore those issues either by yourself, or seek appropriate help/support from a close friend/relative, a mentor, or trusted spiritual guide.

Let's now look at the three remaining aspect of your internal environment and how they affect your ability to develop habits.

Your body

Your body is your physical health, any potential disabilities or special abilities you may have, but also your food and clothing preferences, your sleep patterns, your energy patterns, etc.

Why does it matter? How does it affect your habit-forming attempts?

Some things are quite straightforward and obvious. For instance, if you're trying to develop an exercise routine, your health or fitness level will likely become a source of limitation. Your sleep pattern or your preference for working in the morning/evening may be a limitation and/or a constraint to your schedule.

But don't dismiss less obvious aspects of your body, such as your clothing preferences. For example, if you're working on developing a productivity routine that relies on your phone and you need to move around a lot - are you able to carry the phone in your pocket? Have you got clothes with pockets large enough? If you don't like or are not able to wear clothes with pockets, you'll need to find another strategy for carrying your phone with you, or abandon the idea of relying on your phone.

The same goes for supports and props that belong to this aspect of your context. For example, being a morning person may support you developing a morning exercise regime. Knowing that you feel most comfortable sitting at the kitchen table may serve as a prop to build a productivity routine around it.

These are all things you need to take into consideration when designing your habit-developing or breaking system.

Your mind

Another important source of potential limitations, constraints, as well as supports/props, **your mind** includes **your thinking style, your beliefs, your preferences, personality or interpersonal style**, and very importantly - **other goals you are pursuing.**

To continue using the exercise routine example, your preferences will have a strong impact on your choice of physical activity. Whether you're more likely to stick to an exercise routine if you're doing it on your own or with others would be another important limitation/constraint/support, etc.

Your emotions

Although not always obvious, your emotions may have a powerful effect on your ability to develop a new habit or break an old one.

It may be harder to work on a new productivity routine if

you're going through a stressful period. Regular exercise, on the other hand, may be quite helpful in managing stress. Many people find a recent relationship breakup motivating to start a diet; however, for many this emotional period is too hard to deal with by itself to add anything else that requires self-control.

Be mindful of your emotional state, particularly earlier in the process of forming/breaking a habit. Be mindful of your own reservoir of willpower and stress levels.

Again, depending on your particular situation, your emotional state can work both ways: being a source of constraints and limitations, as well as supports/props.

3. Your Social Environment

Your social environment mainly refers to people directly or indirectly involved in your habit routine.

For example, for productivity routines, most commonly these would be your work colleagues, office mates, or if you work from home - your family or flatmates. But if you like working in cafés, public libraries, or any other public space/communal area, you need to consider other people who may be there at the same time. You don't necessarily have to have specific individuals in mind, but may need to refer to certain groups, depending on your needs, e.g. everybody else using the library/study room at the same time, or whoever sits in the co-working space at the time you're working there.

These will also be people who are indirectly around you when you're working: be it over the phone, via social media, etc. So friends, family, customers, anyone else who may ring you, text you, or post something on Facebook is part of your social environment.

And don't forget all those people in your head. They may have an influence over what you do and how, even though they are not physically there, e.g. your mentors, your girlfriend you can't stop thinking about, all those internal critics, or your critical 'internalised parents.'

Typically, people are aware of the potential positive influence their social environment can provide when developing a new habit.

One of the most common recommendations is to get an accountability buddy or group. Getting your family and friends on board, as well as joining a support group, are also common motivational strategies. Yes, the supports and practical help you can receive from others around you can be a powerful source of energy to push on with your routine on bad days.

But your social context has also a darker side. It may happen that your nearest and dearest not only are unsupportive of your pursuits, but may actively prevent you from taking up certain habits, however good and healthy they may sound. They may feel neglected or excluded when you suddenly start spending time doing something else. And let's not forget the limitations and constraints your social environment imposes on you. What's possible and appropriate may influence your choices and actions particularly strongly, too.

If you work in an open-space office, you are likely to be faced with a number of constraints and limitations of all kinds. Some potential social ones would be:

- If you're sharing a filing cabinet with a colleague, having a filing system just for yourself may not be possible
- If it is, it may not be appropriate to take up all the available space, or use all the folders
- If you want to use noise-cancelling headphones to help you focus on your work, is this appropriate in the context of your company work culture? This may be seen as isolating yourself from your colleagues and hence be discouraged

Obviously, your social networks can be an excellent source of support for you developing better, healthier habits, so don't forget to tap into them.

Time to Take Action

Analyse your context using the table provided in the Workbook. Record your reflections in the appropriate section. Together with the analysis of constraints, limitations, and supports/props available within your internal environment, this will provide a basis for deciding on the Habit Goal to pursue.

In the next chapter we will look at you - your motivational drivers, personality, likes/dislikes, your strengths and weakness, and your other goals - to help you choose the right Habit Goal to pursue to ensure success.

CHAPTER 11:
Know Yourself

One of the most important steps in the process of setting up a fail-proof habit system is a deep and honest understanding of who you are; your personality, your temperament, your strengths and weaknesses. In this chapter we will look at how all these elements can affect your attempts to build better habits and how to put them to work so you can achieve your goals faster.

Let's start with the key issue. You don't need to be a psychologist or see one for advice to work through the steps outlined below. You don't need to do any personality questionnaires. But you do need some knowledge of yourself, and more importantly - **you need to be honest with yourself**.

Complete honesty with yourself is crucial to success. This exercise is not about judging yourself. Nothing is good or bad here. Just as with looking at the external aspects of your context, understanding yourself and the ways you operate will help you avoid previous mistakes and make the change much easier.

Approach this step with honesty and empathy for yourself, but also scientific curiosity. Strip all judgements you may have about yourself. Be mindful of 'I shouldn't be this,' or 'I should be that,' thinking - ban it. It's about the real stuff, the traits of character that are 'default,' the automatic thinking/actions and reactions. The better you understand it, the better your chances at succeeding in this process.

To explore your own personality and temperament, you can use self-reflection. You may want to ask your nearest and dearest for their opinions. Again, it's not about judging yourself or anyone - it's about a deeper understanding of your nature. Write down what they say and keep it handy. You can also use one of the available psychometric tools.

I am not a psychologist, so I cannot make any definite statements of judgement here. But various ability and personality tests and questionnaires exist. Their validity - that is (roughly speaking) their ability to accurately identify what they claim to identify - varies. Some are as good as your first guess; some are more accurate. Some are used in clinical settings, and some for entertainment only.

Use whatever you find helpful and accurate. It's good to get it right the first time around, but even if you don't - it's not a problem. As long as you can easily monitor your progress and tweak your system as appropriate, you can always adjust your course.

The **key personal factors** useful in setting up a fail-proof habit system are:

- **Your personality**, including **your strengths/weaknesses,** your **likes/dislikes,** your **existing routines, customs,** and **quirks**

- **Your motivation**
- **Any other goals you're already pursuing**

In the next section we will look at these factors and how they can affect your habit goal pursuits.

1. Your Personality

Let's look at some aspects of your personality that can affect your ability to build habits and pursue your chosen goal.

Use your strengths and weaknesses

You may have done some personality questionnaires or other tests or explorations intended to help you discover your strengths and weaknesses. You might have suffered, 'tell me about your biggest strength/weakness,' questions at an interview. You may have failed at achieving your goals because of your weakness, or enjoyed many victories thank to your strengths.

Yes, most of it is common sense - if the goal you choose involves you using one of your strengths - that's great - consider it a prop/support.

But if in order to implement it, you'd have to overcome a weakness, or use a skill/ability that's not your forte - it's like having to do something you don't enjoy doing.

And before you say, 'That's okay, I want to work on developing this [skill/ability],' question yourself: Can you afford to invest your time and energy (and maybe money, too) to work on your goal and this [skill/ability] (and many other things) at the same time?

Realistically speaking, having a weakness to overcome/work on before you can achieve your focus goal is a barrier to achieving the goal, and a serious barrier indeed. I'd recommend you review your goal and go through the goal-defining process again.

And now for something that may surprise you.

Knowing your strong and weak points is important to setting up your habit systems, but if you design your system to embrace your biggest weakness - you're onto a winner.

How come?

You're only as strong as your weakest link, if I may paraphrase William James -'A chain is no stronger than its weakest link, and life is after all a chain.'

This quote is the essence of my approach to habit formation and personal change.

And no, I am not talking about working on your weaknesses. Neither am I arguing you should ignore your weaknesses and/or cover/compensate for them with your strengths.

I am saying: **embrace your weaknesses and design your system to RELY on them.**

How well do you think your system would work if it relied on your love of certain foods (e.g. used as a motivator), or your difficulty in social interactions (e.g. going to the gym/swimming pool at antisocial times)?

I dare to guess - rather quite well.

I've successfully used this strategy in numerous habit setups, and hence I believe that as long as your weaknesses are not harmful to anyone or anything, they can be excellent reinforcers of desired behaviours.

Let's say you're trying to improve your productivity and you identified your low threshold for boredom as a weakness. You know your concentration tends to wane after about 20 minutes. You can say it's a weakness and work on extending your attention span - it's a good approach. However, this approach requires some work and it will take time to see results. In the meantime, you may still fail at implementing your focus system and the whole cycle of *motivate yourself – try – push on – fail – motivate yourself*, etc. goes on and on, effecting your self-esteem and your productivity, and exhausting your willpower.

But if you accepted the fact you can focus for 20 minutes at a time and design your work schedule to embrace that, scheduling in short breaks every 20 minutes, then, as long as you stick to those short breaks and make sure the breaks boost your focus rather than further distract you, you can keep going for overall much longer. Yes, it's not an ideal 90-minute block, but if it gets the job done - do you really care?

I don't. That's what I needed to do for myself with my short attention span and low threshold for boredom. And it's kept my system going.

The actual tactics you choose to use your weakness will depend on other aspects of your personality, your other routines, etc. which we will talk about later.

Relying on your weakness to get yourself to do what you want to do every single time is a powerful tool.

Consider your likes and dislikes

When setting up your habit system, you need to consider your likes and dislikes.

This sounds obvious, but many people think they may be able to miraculously overcome a dislike because they have this beautiful, inspirational goal to achieve. All may go well initially, when you're full of good intention and motivation. But when things start getting a bit more difficult, when you're tired, with depleted willpower, guess what happens?

If the goal you've picked requires you to do something you don't like, or stop/do less of what you like - pause and ask yourself the following questions:

How likely are you to carry out this behaviour, knowing you don't like doing it? What would you need to have in place to make it happen most of the time? Can you afford it time-, energy-, and money-wise?

If the answers are clearly telling you the goal would be at risk, reconsider your goal and go through the goal-setting process again.

However, if your goal requires you to do more of what you

like - you're onto a winner.

Use your existing habits, routines, and quirks

As I said many times before, humans are creatures of habit and our lives are run by habits.

Some of those habits are quick, easy routines, such as teeth brushing or putting on your coffee maker. Some are more complex, like your exercise regime, or the weekly shopping trip.

What's important for the success of establishing your new habit system is to understand which of your existing habits and routines you can tap into.

You can use your existing routines in two ways:

- Use an existing habit as an **'anchor habit'** - this is how **keystone habits** often work (keystone habits are habits that have power to transform our lives by creating a culture or environment that enables further changes (1) - I talk more about them in chapter 28.)
- Use an existing habit as **a Cue to your new habit**. The easiest way to use an existing habit is to simply use the current routine as a cue for the new one.

In a nutshell, existing routines can be used as action-based triggers for your new habits. It is important though, to use a well-established routine, something that's well embedded in your daily life, already automated, so you don't have to think about it. If you have a routine that meets this description, try to use is as a Cue for your new habit. For example, if you have a habit of drinking coffee in the morning, you can use your cup-of-coffee routine to trigger a new behaviour - e.g. setting your goals-to-accomplish for today by doing your daily planning while drinking your morning coffee.

You can have a whole series of little actions that stack one after the other to create a more complex, multi-step sequences. Steve 'S.J.' Scott calls this strategy 'habit stacking' (2). Read more about it in chapter 30.

Habit stacking is how I've expanded my morning routine from simply having my coffee and breakfast and studying to adding daily to-do list reviews, keeping track of my business performance, and exercising.

2. Your Motivation

Now, let's look at the driving forces in your life. Motivation is considered to be THE driver of all things in the self-improvement zone. And fair enough - it is. If you think of your goal being your destination, the plan to achieve it and the system you create is your car. Your motivation is obviously the fuel you put in the tank. All good, except one little thing many people forget to consider: what type of fuel does your car take?

There are so many different types of energy we can use to power our vehicles these days: diesel, gasoline, LPG, biofuels, electricity. And you need to know what to put into your tank before you even get into your car. If you put in the wrong fuel, no matter how much you top it up, you aren't going anywhere.

I don't do 'motivational stuff.' As you probably noticed, I think 'motivating yourself' is a very ineffective and wasteful self-improvement strategy. I do, however, believe in the power of getting the right type of fuel into your car - making sure your motivation matches the plan and the system you have built to get to your goal.

Because your motivation is part of your personality it's hard to change. You're either motivated by something or not. It's easier to invest time and effort into discovering what makes you tick, than try to pursue a goal that's misaligned with your motivation. If you choose your goals based on what drives you, you won't need to talk yourself into being motivated by something you don't care about.

There are a number of assessment tools designed to help you figure out what you're motivated by. Many of them are designed for workplaces. However, the good old self-discovery style exercise may be enough.

The key issue is to understand well what makes you tick. Whether it's extrinsic or intrinsic, or a mixture of both, make sure you know what it is. I encourage you to be open, honest, and non-judgemental with yourself when thinking about what motivates you. There are no right or wrong answers. Even though some of the motivators may be frowned upon by others, or even yourself - it is what it is. Check chapter 22 for tips to discover what motivates you.

If your goal is to set up a morning productivity routine because you want to progress in your career, and your underlying motivations are extrinsic, e.g. money, or praise, or power - this is what lights your fire and fuels your desire to achieve your goals. Yes, it may be short-lived as a driver (extrinsic motivators usually are). Yes, many people consider these to be bad or wrong. But if you pretend you're driven by something else, e.g. the need to help others, or the dream of freedom - if these are not real drivers for you, your motivation for achieving your goals will suffer and die out quickly.

3. Your Other Goals

This requires a special mention. A lot of people fail to achieve their goals because they don't consider what else they are pursuing at the same time. A typical example is someone who decides to eat healthier and save money at the same time - healthy eating, which usually requires eating more expensive food, goes against their goal of spending less.

If you have a goal to be more responsive to your customers' phone calls, and at the same time you try to limit distractions, you will have difficulty in trying to achieve both. On the other hand, if you're trying to limit your, 'I need to look for x, y, z,' type of distractions, and you're working on becoming better organised, these are definitely aligned goals, and achieving better organisation will help you reduce the level of mess-generated distractions.

Don't spread yourself too thin

Consider how many goals you're already working towards. You have a limited amount of time and energy. The more you're trying to achieve, the thinner you'll have to spread yourself. But the less you invest in a goal, the less likely you are to achieve it. Studies show that unfinished business takes up 'mental space' and energy and acts as a distractor (Zeigarnik effect (3)). If you're already fully committed, you'd be better off postponing this habit goal, or abandoning a couple of other pursuits, otherwise - you're doomed to fail again.

So think carefully: prioritise, drop before you pick up another goal to pursue, or abandon some goals completely.

Pay attention to conflicting or competing goals

Pay particular attention to any **conflicting or competing goals** - these would put limitations and constraints on the habit goal you are trying to pursue. Ideally, you would want to align your new pursuit with what you're already trying to achieve and hence provide an extra boost to your chances of succeeding at it/both (prop/support).

Knowing yourself is key to successful behavioural change. If you're able to be honest with yourself about what really makes you tick, your previous successes and failures, your weaknesses, likes and dislikes, and other aspects of your personality, and you incorporate this knowledge into your habit-system setup - achieving your goal will be much easier.

Time to Take Action

Now you understand how your personality, motivation, and other goals affect your ability to pursue your chosen Habit Goal, fill in the corresponding parts of the table in the Workbook.

In the next chapter we will look at how you can use your past successes and failures to ensure you achieve your habit goals.

CHAPTER 12:
Use Your Past Successes and Failures to Create Your Winning Strategy

> *'Insanity is doing the same thing over and over again and expecting different results,'* ~ Albert Einstein

Have you ever failed at establishing a habit while using a popular strategy? Are you prone to trying the same approach over and over again, even though it does not seem to get you too far?

Yes, I've been there, too.

I don't meditate, even though I'm fully aware of multiple benefits of meditation.

I've tried meditating many times throughout my life. I have difficulty sitting still for any prolonged period of time. But even if I achieved that desired level of stillness and did not fall asleep or felt uncomfortable, I never experienced enough benefits of meditation to feel it was all worth it. So I've found other ways to improve my focus, memory, keep myself healthy, fit, and happy.

My life-long battles with keeping to a diet are full of examples of insanity as defined above. No matter what I did, how much I tried, how motivated I was, I would always fail around day 3. Now, I know I'm not good at sticking to a diet, and if I want to lose weight I put more emphasis on exercise and limiting sweets than anything else.

The same went for my attempts to establish a regular exercise routine. I didn't succeed at creating an exercise habit until I considered my past patterns of success and failure.

Regardless of what may have worked for others in similar situations, regardless of what all sorts of 'gurus' may have told you - common sense should always prevail. Don't repeat old mistakes by employing strategies that have not worked in the past.

And, similarly, don't push yourself to use popular strategies that have proven ineffective for you, even if they've helped millions of others. Unless your context has changed.

My approach to successful habit system creation takes your past successes and failures into consideration. It's common sense: avoid ineffective strategies and build upon things that have worked for you in the past.

1. Analyse Your Failures to Discover Ineffective Strategies

First, let's focus on avoiding repeating the old mistakes.

Think of your previous unsuccessful attempts to establish this habit in the past.

Whether you've failed completely at establishing your habit, or were doing well until you gave it up, look at the reasons. Why did you fail/gave up? What were the obstacles in your environment? Was it something in your internal world (your emotions, your thinking patterns)? Or maybe in your social network?

The earlier chapters in this part (Know Your Context, Know Yourself) will help you identify various aspects of your context that may have contributed to your difficulties/failures.

These may be your weaknesses, your shortcomings, skill or experience gaps, your likes and dislikes, your personal situation at the time, such as:

- Getting the motivation part wrong, e.g. doing something to please someone, or doing something you didn't care about
- Setting yourself an unrealistic goal, such as losing 30kg in 30 days or resolving to exercise before work, when you're an owl and you know you struggle to get up earlier
- Deciding to do something you don't like parts/elements or the total of, e.g. to go to the gym when you don't like exercising indoors and with people around you

Be as honest as you possibly can. Don't judge yourself. Put your scientific discovery hat on and go exploring with curiosity, not shame, blame, or pride. The better you understand what has stopped you from achieving your goals so far, the better prepared for the journey ahead you will be.

If this is your first attempt at creating this specific habit, think of times when you did not succeed at establishing other habits. You can go through this exercise also as an extension to the previous part.

2. Look at What's Worked for You in the Past

Do the same for all your successful attempts. If you have achieved establishing the same habit in the past, analyse your success in the way described in the section on failures. However, if you haven't succeeded at this particular habit in the past, or this is your first attempt, analyse your other successes with other behavioural changes - as big or as little as you want. Look again at the strategies you used, and the reasons that contributed to your success.

3. Analyse Your Past Successes and Failures for Patterns

Once you have captured the reasons for not achieving your habit goals in the past, look for patterns. Try to group these causes into larger, more generalised, or higher-level items. For example, you may notice that you tend to give up your new routine on weekends because your weekend days lack the structure your weekdays have. You may see that every time you've tried to introduce a new behaviour in the evening, it did not last long. It may also be that you can see which aspects of your personality may get in the way; for instance, the fact you are an owl and prefer to work in the evenings or late at night, or you are an introvert who prefers to do things on your own.

I did this analysis when establishing my new exercise routine. As I mentioned earlier, I run three times a week, even though I hate running. But from my past failures I knew I don't stick to a rigid routine, hence anything that requires me to start and finish at a certain time was out (e.g. gym classes, some swimming sessions). I hate driving and in the past anything that meant driving to the place where I exercise was always at risk of failure. I also know that doing anything that relied on other people turning up, having time, motivation, etc. was not a good strategy. I have always been good at doing stuff regularly if I had some flexibility in the schedule, no other people to consider (I'm an introvert) and not much fuss and gear to get ready. Once I'd taken all that into consideration, the choice was easy - walking or running. Since I walk a lot anyway, I don't consider it exercise, so I settled on running and have been successfully running regularly for over a year now.

Time to Take Action

Write down the type of habit you tried to establish and failed at. Then, describe the strategy/strategies you used. Reflect on the reasons why it went wrong and write them down, too.

Do the same for successful strategies. Remember, you are looking for patterns here. You can start with writing down every single cause or internal obstacle you think caused you to give up or fail your habit goals, but try to group them into more generalised themes.

Record your reflections in the Workbook.

Now, you have a good understanding of what elements of

your context, what strategies, and what aspects of your personality and motivation can help or hinder your establishing your habit system. That's a huge job. Well done. In the next chapter I'll show you how to set a Habit Goal.

Part 4:

DESIGN YOUR HABIT SYSTEM

- Chapter 13: Pick a Cue
- Chapter 14: Map out Your Routine
- Chapter 15: Choose Your Reward
- Chapter 16: Put Your Habit Loop and Habit Plan Together
- Chapter 17: How to Break an Old Habit

HACK YOUR HABITS

Chapter 13:
Pick a Cue

So now you know how habits work, and how your own context - your environment and yourself - can influence the process of habit formation.

Next, we will look at setting up your own habit system, using the three-element habit loop: Cue - Routine - Reward.

All that hard work you have done will now be put into practice, so you can reap the benefits of a routine that's easy to implement and stick to.

We'll start with **the Cue.**

When you walk to the bathroom in the morning and see your toothbrush - do you grab it and proceed to brushing? Or do you pause to think, 'Oh, I'd better check if my teeth need cleaning... I need that tingling sensation in my mouth that indicates they're clean.'

I'd guess you don't really think about it anymore. It's so well engrained in your brain that the process is automatic.

A habit is formed when we stop paying attention to the connection between the action (teeth brushing) and the outcome (the sensation of having clean teeth), and start responding to the stimulus in the environment (I see the toothbrush - I clean my teeth). (1)

This is the state we're after: responding to the Cue rather than going through the whole thinking process.

Cue is the first step of this cycle, and the key to successful habit formation is finding a Cue that will trigger the desired action every time you see, hear, smell, or feel it.

How to Find an Effective Cue

Finding a good Cue is one of the two key elements of establishing a successful habit. A traditional approach to finding Cues (3, 4) is to base them on time, preceding activity, location, other people, or emotional state.

In my experience of establishing a multitude of smaller and bigger habits as well as helping other people do it, the most effective Cues are those that are always there when you need to perform the new behaviour. It is something you can clearly notice and is hard to ignore. It does not necessarily mean it needs to be huge or loud, but it needs to cut through the info noise around you. What works best is a Cue that 'disrupts your reality.'

I'm quite clumsy and often get hurt because of that, particularly around the kitchen. I used to burn my fingers on the hot oven a lot, until I came up with this little idea: when the oven is hot, the light is on. So I put the oven on and turn the light on at the same time. But I don't turn the light off when I turn the oven off. I leave it on until the oven is cool enough to be safe. I know when the light is on - the oven is hot. And my family knows it, too. I am convinced this little system is the reason why my daughter didn't have an unpleasant encounter with the hot oven as a kid.

So the light in the oven 'disrupts my reality' - I know something is not quite right.

I did the same thing when getting into a habit of logging my runs - on returning from a run, before heading off for a shower, I would take my fitness tracker off (not waterproof) and leave it on top of my laptop. So when I was back from the bathroom - the tracker on the laptop was a sign I had to log my run. I couldn't open the laptop without doing something with the tracker.

I encourage my clients to find a Cue that really gets in the way of performing what would be the old behaviour (e.g. opening the laptop and just getting on with my work, in my case, and forgetting to log my run yet again), or that stops/slows you down so that you can remember what you wanted to do.

One of the students of my Laser-Sharp Focus on Autopilot course at www.theshapeshiftersclub.com/focus came up with the idea of putting a big corkboard where he kept track of his productivity routines on the table so that it blocked his access to his computer. In order to access the computer, he had to remove the board and do something with it. A big board is not easy to just shift in a second - you need time to do that. For him, it was enough to remind him what the board was there for and start his productivity routine.

While calendar reminders seem like a great idea, they often

don't work because it's very easy to ignore them, or just 'snooze' them. We become blind/deaf to notifications - there are so many of them around us.

1. Using Environment-Based Cues

The best Cues are those located in the environment where you perform the desired behaviour, and those that are difficult to ignore. These Cues are **already in your 'habit space:' furniture, tools,** and **other gear** needed to carry out the desired action **work best.**

If you're building a productivity routine, plant a Cue on your desk, within your workspace. I use a little notebook and pen duo as a bookmark when reading self-development books - it's an excellent prompt that I want to take notes from the book.

If you're trying to develop a regular exercise regime, consider using your workout clothes or gear as a Cue. Some people leave their sport shoes by their bed or exit from the bedroom, so they trip over them when they get out of bed on their workout days.

Be creative, think outside the box. Don't be shy or embarrassed to try stuff that's really unusual (just remember don't harm anyone or yourself, and don't do to others what you wouldn't want them to do to you). There are a multitude of solutions if you're prepared to be open about them. The most effective solutions are often unusual - because they stand out so much from the usual environment they are bound to work.

Visual Cues work really well, particularly if your new

behaviour is linked with a particular space - whether it's your workspace for your productivity routine, your bedroom for exercise in the morning, or your fridge when you're trying to eat healthier.

Cues that are part of your environment are there regardless of the time, so if you happen to get up 10 minutes later or earlier, your Cue - your running shoes - are still there by your bed waiting for you to put them on, so you don't forget about it.

As long as you're at that place, you can see the reminder and you'll know what you're supposed to do.

What to do if you don't have a single habit space

This gets a bit more complicated if you are required to carry out your new behaviour in various places. This is a common scenario for knowledge workers who work from different locations. You have two solutions:

- Plant a Cue in every single one of those spaces
- Carry the Cue with you

If you have a limited, but stable number of places where you need your routine to kick in, you may want to invest in **having separate Cues for all of these spaces**. Solving the problem may be as simple as reproducing the same Cue in every one of those spaces. However, due to the different nature of those environment/contexts as well as the different nature of work you need to carry out in different spaces, sometimes you may need to design different Cues for different spaces.

Alternatively, you can **carry the Cue with you**. Most commonly people use their phones (the reminder function on their phones) as a way to cue themselves. This may work well if you're already 'conditioned' to pay attention to reminder notifications. However, if you happen to be habituated, there is little point in using a Cue you're likely to ignore.

Again, the tool(s) or gear you need to complete the behaviour you're supposed to perform work really well. If you want to break your habit of signing documents without properly reading them - you can try to use your pen as a Cue to slow/stop yourself (e.g. by carrying a pen that doesn't work, so you need to find a working one, which gives you time to pause before you complete the old automated behaviour).

2. When Environment-Based Cues Don't Work for You

If, for whatever reason, the environment-based cue doesn't work for you, you can try the other strategies:

Time-based Cue

Use a time-based Cue when you are on a schedule and are generally a schedule-loving person. If you're a little more relaxed about it, this may not work as well for you. Snoozing that popup notification too often is likely to turn into 'notification habituation' and notification blindness.

Time-based Cues work well if you're organised and have a

schedule. Use the calendar function on your devices to serve you reminders. For the best results - use the same system across all the devices you use and make sure the devices synchronise.

Preceding activity-based Cue

Assuming that the preceding activity is already well anchored in your routine, preceding activity-based Cues work well. They work best in habit-stacking situations mentioned in Chapters 11 and 30.

This is how I got myself to floss my teeth regularly every evening after brushing my teeth. I also used my teeth brushing routine to incorporate feet exercises, when I had problems with my feet.

Emotional state-based Cues

These Cues can be very useful when breaking old habits that try to address an emotional issue. Due to their nature, they can be difficult to master, as powerful emotional states usually result in 'brain hijack' (4), which is harder to handle.

Person-based Cues

These may be useful when you're working on your behaviour that is specific to social situations. For example, if you're trying to talk to people more, or gossip less.

Whichever type of Cue you use, make sure it always (or almost always) works for you. Test it and don't be afraid of dumping a Cue that's not delivering. The better your Cue, the easier it will be to stick to your behaviour, so invest time and effort into getting this part right.

Time to Take Action

Think about the setting where you will perform your new Routine: be it the gym for your exercise routine, or your desk/office for your productivity routine, or maybe your interactions with your team members. Consider whether you can use anything already in the environment as the cue for your new behaviour. If you can't use your environment, consider the alternatives: time-based, preceding activity, emotional state, or person-based. What kind of Cue would work best in your case?

Write down your choice of the Cue in the Workbook.

Next, we will look at mapping out your Routine.

CHAPTER 14:
Map out Your Routine

Routine is the actual action(s) you take to achieve the Habit Goal you came up with in Chapter 9. Below are the steps that can help you build the Routine.

1. Start with Your Habit Goal

Your Routine will depend on the specific Habit Goal you have identified earlier and recorded in your Workbook.

With that in mind, think of a simple behaviour you can do every day, or in some other regular pattern, an action that would take you closer to your habit goal.

If you're building an exercise habit, you may come up with the idea of a daily yoga session or running 3 times per week.

If you're working towards being more productive, this may be what you do to reduce technology distractions.

If you're trying to stop yourself from yelling at your kids - this may be the action you take every time you feel like yelling at them.

2. Describe Your Action in Detail

As with any other goal, the clearer you are about what you need to do, the more likely you are to follow the process.

What is it what you want to do, or do instead of your old behaviour?

If you're trying to eliminate technology distractions, you may decide to turn off all the notifications as soon as you sit down to work.

If you feel like shouting at your kids, you may decide to take 3 deep breaths instead.

And if your new behaviour consists of several little steps, make sure you break it down into those steps.

3. Write it All Down – As a Checklist

As your Cue serves a reminder of **when** to perform an action, the checklist helps you remember **what** to do.

At some point, your new actions will become automatic - and this is the moment when your new behaviour becomes - well, a habit. Unfortunately, it takes time for the new Routine to embed into your life. What, then, should you do to help yourself get to the point when your habit becomes automatic without constantly defaulting on your desired behaviour?

Here's my tip:

Don't rely on your memory. It's already unreliable, and the

heavier the cognitive load on it, the more likely you are to forget what you were to do, or make mistakes (1).

The best way of recording the steps is by creating a step-by-step checklist. Checklists not only reduce cognitive load, but also help us focus on things that we need to do and do them in the right order.

They are very effective, across many industries, e.g. in healthcare checklists help prevent many infections, and hence not only save a lot of money, but also save lives. (2)

Research shows that if you follow a checklist, you're 75% less likely to miss any of the steps required - and reduce the likelihood of failure to carry out your desired behaviour from 23% to 6% (3).

When creating a checklist:

- Focus on critical steps and use as few steps as possible (the more steps you have, the more intimidating the checklist looks and the less likely you are to follow the steps)
- Ideally, you want it to fit on one page (my checklists need to fit on a standard size post-it note - no room for writing novels.)
- Make sure the sequence of steps fits the flow of your behaviour (e.g. don't turn your fitness tracker on before you put your running shoes on)
- Use simple sentences and basic language
- Make sure it's visible and easy to read (font/colour etc.)

For your exercise session it may be something like this:

1. Put on my workout clothes
2. Grab my water bottle
3. Grab my mp3 player and put on my favourite music
4. Turn on Workout setting in my fitness tracker
5. Run for 30 minutes

4. Transfer Your Checklist onto a Suitable Medium

Once you've got it all recorded, think of the best medium to put your checklist onto. I found that having a checklist with all the steps easily available at the time I'm supposed to carry out my new Routine is very helpful. Ideally, I recommend that you keep it together with your Cue for this particular Routine (e.g. a productivity routine checklist may be placed on your desk, your workout routine under your mp3 player, etc.).

For example, when I first started getting into my focus routine, I had the checklist written on a little post-it note and attached it to the cover of my laptop. The post-it served as a Cue and a checklist for the Routine at the same time. Every time I was to sit down and work, I'd open my laptop, obviously spotting the post-it first. This would prompt me to carry out my focus routine and make sure I had everything needed within reach, closed unnecessary programs/apps, etc.

So keep your checklist in your pocket, on your phone, pinned on the board over your desk - where you can easily access it and use it just when you need to.

Time to Take Action

Look back at your Habit Goal. Now, your task is to come up with a simple, daily/regular action that will take you closer to your Habit Goal. This is something you want to implement into your life as a new Routine. Break it down into simple steps and create a checklist. Record it in the Workbook.

Transcribe your checklist onto a suitable medium if necessary.

HACK YOUR HABITS

CHAPTER 15:
Choose Your Reward

In this chapter we'll zero in on rewards. Because while Cue can help you perform the desired behaviour, it's the Reward that keeps the loop going.

The Reward is what makes you want, (yes, WANT) to come back for more.

Rewards make the habit. They make us 'addicted' to those behaviours that we keep carrying out in the anticipation of reward.

If you want to set a successful habit system, make sure you have a good reward to keep you coming back for more.

What is a Reward?

Rewards are objects, situations, impulses, or events that directly or indirectly lead to the activation of pleasure centres in our brain. To put it simply - rewards (and anticipation of rewards) are what makes us feel good.

Rewards can be intrinsic - acting directly on our pleasure centres, or extrinsic - the ones that work indirectly, through learnt associations.

Rewards keeps us 'hooked' on the behaviours that bring them

or even only promise them.

That's why rewards are powerful motivators.

Rewards can be different for different people and their effect on us can change over time. Different people are driven by different things. What makes me tick may not work for you and vice versa. Also, because we all change and adapt to the environment around us, what used to motivate us when we were younger may no longer be of interest/benefit, and hence no longer effective as a Reward.

Types of Rewards

Typically Rewards, like motivators, can be divided into two types:

Extrinsic rewards

Extrinsic rewards are external to us, such as monetary and other material rewards (money, but also equivalents such as points, gifts), praise (making someone proud of you, getting that 'employee of the month' or 'best student' title, but also good grades, honourable mentions, etc.), as well as avoidance of punishment (direct, e.g. fines, 'naming and shaming,' getting fired, but also avoiding social exclusion or someone's anger, etc.)

Intrinsic rewards

Intrinsic rewards come from within us, such as the sense of autonomy, mastery, and purpose.

How to Use Rewards to Build a Successful Habit System

This is how you can use your understanding of rewards to help you set up a successful habit system:

1. Use what motivates you to reinforce your habit cycle

The best way to reward yourself for the desired behaviour is to use things that really make you tick.

Obvious, isn't it? Give yourself a Reward you really care about.

You would be surprised to know how many people try rewarding themselves with stuff they don't give damn about, or are only mildly interested in.

Examples? Lily, who I wrote about in Chapter 3. Yes, being healthy and fit is an awesome goal, except... when you don't really care about being healthy and fit. It may sound strange; of course we're all motivated to survive, and being healthy and fit is the best survival strategy. And that's what Lily thought when she first set herself a weight-loss goal.

Then, she realised it didn't really bother her that much. It didn't work until her poor fitness, and to some extent weight, started to have a significant impact on her ability to be independent - affecting her autonomy - the thing she really did care about. Within a couple of months, she shed a few pounds and became fitter.

No, scrap that: within a couple of months she overcome her

difficulty in mobilising and ended up losing some weight and improving her fitness levels. Goal achieved.

What made the difference? The fact that she rewarded herself by tracking her improving independence/autonomy, rather than how much weight she lost or how many steps she made, which did not really matter to her.

Whether you're driven by money and fame, or wanting world peace - make sure the Reward you attach to your habit matches what you care about. This principle applies to both intrinsic and extrinsic rewards.

2. Use extrinsic and intrinsic Rewards wisely

Intrinsic rewards are best not only because they affect our pleasure centres directly, but also because they are effective long term.

Intrinsic rewards are often what drives us through life, our passions and personal missions.

They are very effective and powerful.

Unfortunately, extrinsic rewards are trickier. For starters, these are often things and situations we learnt to associate with the Reward, but are not directly involved in releasing that 'feel good' feeling. Also, after a while, their effectiveness wears off. Worse, in the long run, extrinsic rewards used to reinforce a behaviour that would otherwise come from within (intrinsically) can significantly undermine the intrinsic driver and the person's interest in the behaviour (1) (this is also known as the over-justification effect (2)).

This is why it's important to use extrinsic rewards carefully.

But don't write off extrinsic rewards completely. While intrinsic rewards work well in the long run, there will be times when your intrinsic motivation will be down, and you'll still need to get the job done.

This is particularly true early in the process of habit formation - once the initial excitement is over and the new behaviour has not yet become automatic. This is when extrinsic rewards come handy.

It may also be useful to use extrinsic rewards on bad days - when you're stressed, tried, with limited willpower, and at any other point you feel your intrinsic motivation to carry on has gone 'on holidays.'

So:

- Make sure your habit system is fuelled by an intrinsic motivator and be clear what your intrinsic reward is
- Use extrinsic rewards mainly early on, carefully and sparsely
- Be careful not to use extrinsic rewards where you have intrinsic motivation overall
- Reward yourself smartly

To make sure your Rewards work to the best of their ability, consider the following **patterns of rewarding** as these approaches have been proven most effective (3):

- Initially the desired behaviour is rewarded every time it's performed and immediately afterward, so the link between the behaviour and the Reward is clear. However, once our brain figures out this is what's going to happen, the Reward loses its effectiveness. In this situation, it may be time to deploy another strategy.

- Reward is given in an unpredictable pattern. This is the most powerful manner in which Rewards can be put to work. It's well exploited by casinos and other gambling settings, as well as games. If the player does not know when the next Reward is coming, he/she is always hoping it is around the corner and believes that, 'Next time I'm sure I'll hit the jackpot,' or 'I'll solve this level and get to the next one.'

Interestingly, irregular rewarding explores the power of **the promise of reward**, which can be as strong as the reward itself in enticing us to pursue the desired behaviour.

Initially, what you want is to get the habit loop embedded into your life. That's why you may need to reward yourself every time until it becomes easier and more automatic. As your Routine gets established you will need to decrease the frequency of Rewards, and also the type (extrinsic vs. intrinsic), because you're most likely to use extrinsic rewards and the effect of them wears off with time.

What to Use as Rewards

This part may be obvious to you, but many people have actually asked me what they should use as Rewards.

My approach to it is simple and pragmatic: whatever works for you, as long as it doesn't harm you or anyone else.

Just make sure it really matters to you, it really gives you that sense of pleasure, and that you link it with your new behaviour.

Extrinsic rewards are quite straightforward: food is a commonly used Reward (I will not comment on the negative aspects of it here - use your own judgement). It may also be a round of your favourite game (this is what I do when I do such dreaded tasks as proofreading my writing, or preparing my tax returns).

What may be more challenging is to translate your intrinsic motivation into Rewards.

An Alternative Approach to Rewards – Temptation Bundling

Temptation building is a term coined by Katherine Milkman, a Wharton School professor, who first discovered the usefulness of this approach a few years ago when struggling to go to the gym on regular basis. Milkman tested the strategy first on herself, and then on other people (4) and it's been proven quite effective.

The idea is that you're allowed to indulge in your 'guilty pleasures' only when you're carrying out your desired behaviour. I'm sure many of you have used it before - listening to your favourite music on your mp3 player while working out, or watching your favourite show in the gym. This is how a friend of mine gets through a pile of ironing - she would only do that while listening to her favourite songs and singing (at her family's request she's not allowed to sing in the house otherwise).

I used a similar strategy to schedule my exercise sessions before I came up with my current routine. I would go to the gym or swimming on days when I had to wash my hair. I hate washing my hair, but I know I have to do it. I hated going to the gym and although I love swimming, I don't like the hassle of having to wash yourself, hair included, afterwards. So combining these two 'I hate it' tasks was quite effective as a motivator.

I've heard of temptation bundling being used as a way to manage weight-loss programs: you can only have a piece of cake/indulge in some sort of 'guilty food' if you've done x amount of exercise today.

Temptation bundling can be quite effective, if you deploy it smartly. Make sure you pair your desired behaviour with a little indulgence you really care about but would otherwise not allow yourself (e.g. cake while you're on a diet with an exercise session; or watching a TV program while doing something productive, such as housework or exercise). Also use it with the purpose in mind - be aware that you employ this particular strategy with the view to rewarding yourself and treat it like a treat. Most importantly - don't overdo it and don't undermine or cancel the positive effects of your Routine.

Promise of Reward

This may come as a surprise to you, but once your brain has been 'trained' to respond to certain Rewards, it will start responding to anticipation of reward in a similar way as to the Reward itself (5).

That's why promising yourself a Reward that you know you enjoy may be just enough to get you going.

Since I learnt about this phenomenon, I've tested it a number of times. It has worked quite nicely with the Rewards I know are effective for me - food, and sweets in particular. But what's really interesting about the promise of reward is that you promise yourself the Reward with the full intention of getting it, but when the time comes you consider if you still want it. And if you give yourself enough time to think before you act, you may actually see yourself thinking, 'Oh, well actually I don't really want it.'

So this is how you can use Rewards to keep your new habit system going.

Don't be afraid of experimenting with various Rewards until you find the one that consistently makes you come back for more. But beware of the power of it - use your judgement and don't do any harm to yourself or anyone else.

If you noticed you're 'hooked' on the Reward (or behaviour) so much it took over you and you lost control, or if you experience any negative effect of your actions, seek appropriate help - talk to your family doctor.

Time to Take Action

Identify effective Rewards for you. Start with your intrinsic motivation and the specific driver for the habit change you're pursuing and consider how you can include it into your Habit Loop.

Think also of effective extrinsic rewards and ways you can use them with your new habit.

Once you've identified your Rewards, write them down in your workbook. Then, think of the best ways of rewarding yourself - straight after you completed your Routine, or maybe as a temptation bundle, or promise of reward?

Record it in the Workbook.

In the next chapter we'll look at putting it all together and putting the system into action.

CHAPTER 16:
Put Your Habit Loop and Habit Plan Together

So far, we have covered the three elements of the habit loop: Cue, Routine, and Reward. Now we will look at putting the whole Habit Loop together. Your work recorded in your Workbook will help you build it, so keep it handy.

1. Prepare all the Elements of the Loop

By now, you should have all three elements of the Habit Loop identified:

- Cue
- Routine
- Reward

2. Connect Your Cue with Your Routine

Remember that the Cue's main job is to prompt you to carry out your Routine. The closer you have these two elements connected, the better it will work.

Just as I mentioned in Chapter 13, the best approach is to have your Cue either already part of your habit environment or one of the tools, part of your work gear/kit that you're certain to have accessible every time you need to carry out your new Routine.

Ideally, you want your Cue to lead immediately to your Routine. This may be made possible if your Routine checklist is connected to your Cue or it *is* your Cue.

The best examples of the connection Cue - Routine will be post-it notes with the Routine steps/checklist written on them, or a phone reminder with the checklist/steps included.

If this is technically not possible, try to put your Routine description as close to the Cue as possible, just like in the examples I gave you in Chapter 14.

3. Connect Your Reward

Think of what, when, and how you're going to reward yourself for carrying out the Routine.

4. Write Down How You're Going to Do It

Now, you've got all the elements, let's look at the best, most effective way of making sure it works.

The strategy that's been proven to work in habit formation and behaviour change goals (1,2) is called **implementation intention** (3). The implementation intention approach helps you create plans for all the instances when you want to carry out your new behaviour.

So now, think of the entire sequence: from Cue - through Routine - to Reward, and note:

- What you will be doing - step by step
- When
- Where
- How

Use the Workbook to help you formulate your own **Habit Plan**

For the exercise session example described in chapter 14 prompted by a phone reminder, this may be:

Every Tuesday, Thursday, and Saturday morning, when the reminder pops up on my phone, I will put on my running gear, grab my water bottle and my mp3 player, turn on the Workout button on my fitness tracker, and go for a run in the local park. I will reward myself with 30 minutes of playing my favourite game on my tablet.

If you want to develop a productivity habit where you eliminate distractions, your implementation intention plan may look something like:

Every morning when I sit at my desk to work, I will turn off all the notifications, close all the unnecessary applications, turn off the sound and any source of noise in the office, and then tackle task number 1 on my to-do list. I will reward myself with a coffee break once I've done the first task.

You can find a template to help you create a **Habit Plan** in the Workbook.

5. Be Patient

It takes time to create habits and automate them.

Brains and human nature take time to change. Studies have shown it can take anything between 18 days to 7-8 months to put a new behaviour on automatic pilot (4). The length of time depends on the complexity of the habit, and the difficulty of the change - which is individual and will depend on your context and how well you've prepared yourself to implement the change.

My system aims at shortening the length of time it takes, and I have achieved an overnight change, but the best policy is to accept it will take however much time it needs. Being patient and continuing with your practice is key to developing an automated behaviour.

Faced with this amount of uncertainty, just accept it will take time to get into the habit of a new habit.

6. Just Show Up

Remember, building habits is about creating a system, rather than aiming for a specific level of performance. At first, this is all about 'showing up' - practice. It doesn't matter that you're not really good at it (after all, you've just started). Don't worry about the quality or quantity of your output - just make sure you carry out the behaviour every time you are scheduled to do it, and the performance will come later.

7. Signs Your new Behaviour is Becoming Automated

There will be a point when your new behaviour will become automatic. Here are the signs to look out for (as described by Stephen Guise in his Mini Habits book (6)):

- You pay less attention to the outcome of your activity and just 'get on with it' in response to the stimulus (e.g. when you get up in the morning and trip over your running shoes, you just put them on and get ready to go out for your run rather than thinking about what the shoes by the bed mean and trying to 'motivate yourself' to go for your run) (5)
- Your resistance to the activity is diminishing (you just get on with it)
- You pay less attention to the activity itself; ultimately you do it without thinking about it
- Your new routine becomes normal, part of everyday activities, and hence does not evoke emotions anymore (I used to hate running, I still find it boring, but I no longer feel emotional about it)
- The habit becomes part of who you are, how you operate, 'the way you roll' (6)

Time to Take Action

In this chapter we've looked at putting the Habit Loop together and creating a Habit Plan. Now, it's time for you to take action.

Grab your Workbook and use the templates provided to

create the Habit Loop and a Habit Plan.

Next, we'll look at the process for breaking an existing, unwanted habit. There are a lot of similarities, but there are also some key differences.

CHAPTER 17:
How to Break an Old Habit

The process we have discussed so far is based on developing a new habit from scratch. But what should you do if you have a bad habit you want to change?

First of all, I wanted to mention that all of the previously discussed principles still apply here: the habit loop, the role that the Cue plays, the importance of choosing the right Reward, and the principles for setting up your Habit Plan. The main difference is the sequence of events.

It's Easier to Change a Bad Habit Than to Eliminate it

Habits serve a purpose. All of them, even the bad ones.

I've got a bad habit of chewing the caps on my pens off - I chewed through a good few dozens of them, making some of them completely unusable. I tried to stop a few years ago. I succeeded, but then I acquired a habit of snacking.

Well, I didn't really 'acquire snacking' - I reverted to it, because chewing pens had been a substitute for snacking for some time. So, I then tried chewing gum, but it didn't quite do the trick. I considered the pros and cons of snacking versus chewing pens and

I've gone back to destroying pens.

What a vicious circle.

Nature abhors a vacuum, says the ancient saying attributed to Aristotle (1), and this seems to be particularly true when it comes to human nature and habits. If all our habits have purpose, if you get rid of one, your body and mind will try to return to equilibrium by replacing the old habit with another one that will serve the same purpose.

Obviously, destroying pens was not the purpose of my habit. It seems like it was something to do with chewing. Or maybe not...

The process to successfully change or break a bad habit is as follows:

1. Discover What Your Bad Habit Does For You

As James Clear writes (2), habits are in our life for a reason. The key to successfully changing a habit is to have a good understanding of the role it plays in your life.

My pen-chewing habit is a way of dealing with stress and helping me concentrate when I'm struggling to focus on a task. It's the act of chewing that helps - for whatever reason I find chewing helpful.

I'm not unique in my difficulties. Again, James Clear, habit-mastery expert, argues that most bad habits are born as a way of dealing with stress or boredom (2).

I'm sure many of you can relate to my overeating, or pen/nails-chewing when stressed or playing/procrastinating when bored/under stimulated at work. Some of you will be well acquainted with other bad habits born out of stress - shouting at your kids when they're not ready for school, swearing when under pressure, or out of boredom: such as mindless eating, drinking or binge-watching TV.

Remember - those bad habits serve a purpose, too. Don't try to simply eradicate them, because the underlying need will remain unmet. And your clever mind will find another way of ensuring the need is met - by introducing another bad habit.

Invest time and effort into finding out what your habit is helping you with. It may be hard to see any positives in your bad habit, but stay open-minded and curious when exploring it. Look at the most common scenarios when your undesired behaviour happens: is it under stress or when you're bored? You may be able to further narrow down the specific type of stress that causes you to resort to the habit.

My chewing habit is a way of coping with situations when I have to focus on the task at hand when I'm stressed, and it's usually in the context of writing an important document, such as a legal report, or a particularly tricky assessment, or even a potentially inflammatory email reply.

2. Replace Your Habit with a New Behaviour and Address the Underlying Need

Once you've figured out what the old habit does for you, address the underlying cause, or think of other, acceptable ways in which your need can be met.

Remember, if you just address the action, which is in fact helping you deal with something else, the underlying problem will still need some solution. And if you're not careful, if you ignore it, your subconscious will find a way to fill the gap - with another bad habit. For example, if you are putting off working on your assignments because you don't feel confident in your essay-writing skills and it stresses you, you may schedule your assignment-working sessions earlier, but you will still struggle with the same anxiety until you address the underlying skill or knowledge gap. So find out what the source of your behaviour is and try to address it in a healthier way.

However, if you can't eliminate or address the need in another way, find a different action that would meet your need but in a less damaging, or more acceptable way.

If you're trying to not to shout at your kids when you're under pressure to be ready for school on time, you may look at ways to eliminate that morning pressure. However, it may not be completely in your power to do so, hence you may need another way of dealing with the situation, e.g. by telling your kids to hurry up but without yelling at them.

Since I couldn't eliminate the stress of writing important reports or tricky email replies from my work life, I decided to address the need to stay focused. So I went from snacking (weight gain), to pen-chewing (costly), to snacking again (weight gain again), to gum-chewing (not effective) to chewing on a silicon ring. Yes, I got one of those teething rings. Luckily, I found one that doesn't make any noise. And that works a treat. I do need to keep it private, because people do look at me strangely.

3. Experiment with Various Rewards

Interestingly, finding out what the Reward should be comes before figuring out the Cue in this Habit Loop. I was surprised when I first read about it in Charles Duhigg's book (3). But once I thought about it, it all made sense.

We carry out our habitual actions because we want the Reward. In the context of bad habits, the feeling of the underlying need being met is often at least part of that. So relief from boredom or stress is rewarding. Sometimes there will be more to it, so it's important to identify more than one solution and test them.

I've tried chewing gum, but it was not satisfying enough and I reverted to other unhealthy or costly ways of dealing with the issue. But the teething ring has proven to be a good solution - a satisfying Reward, so to speak.

Once you figure out what need your bad habit fulfils, find ways of rewarding yourself in a way that addresses the underlying need. Experiment with various Rewards to check what works best for you.

4. Identify the Cue

Yes, it's the same old Habit Loop, but this time, you need to identify what it is that prompts you to kick-start the undesirable habit.

For my chewing habit, it was the feeling of being overwhelmed and having a 'blank mind,' and the action of turning my gaze away from the computer monitor to find something to chew on. The feeling of being overwhelmed is hard for me to pinpoint, but the action of reaching for something to chew on is unmistakable. That's why I decided to use that action as my Cue.

Your Cues are likely to be linked with (3)

- Your state of mind/emotional state
- Your location
- The time of day
- Other people around you
- The preceding action

5. Use Your Cue as the Prompt for the New Behaviour

Once you've nailed down the Cue, like with other habits, use it to prompt you to carry out your new behaviour - the one that you identified above.

So every time you feel like shouting at your kids to hurry up, otherwise you'll all be late, you open mouth can be your Cue- and your new behaviour may be: taking a deep breath, counting to 6 in your mind, and then telling them to hurry up in a calm but assertive voice.

6. Create a Habit Plan

Just like with other habits discussed earlier, once you have all three elements Cue - Routine - Reward, think of other important aspects of a successful Habit Plan, such as implementation intention, etc. Follow the instructions presented in Chapter 16.

Time to Take Action

If you're looking at breaking an old habit, don't just try to eliminate it - replace it with a good, or at least neutral, one. Think of the underlying issues, the need(s) that the undesired habit meets and find other ways of meeting your need.

Go through the Habit Loop discovery in the sequence described above and write it all down.

Create a Habit Plan just as you would do for a new habit (see chapter 16 for tips on how to do it).

HACK YOUR **HABITS**

Part 5:

FAIL AND FUTURE-PROOF YOUR SYSTEM

- Chapter 18: 5 Strategies to Help You Kick Temptations
- Chapter 19: 5 Ways to Kill Resistance Upfront
- Chapter 20: Guest Expert Chapter – Stephen Guise - Mini-Habits Strategy for Personal Development
- Chapter 21: Test, Track, Tweak and Celebrate Your Progress

HACK YOUR **HABITS**

Chapter 18:
5 Strategies to Help You Kick Temptations

> *'To succeed at self-control, you need to know how you fail.'* (1)
> ~Kelly McGonigal

Have you ever cringed watching talent show auditions, wondering, 'Do those people have no clue they can't even sing in tune?'

We tend to overestimate our abilities in many areas, including multitasking, singing talents, sense of humour, reasoning skills, and - ability to resist temptations. This cognitive bias has been researched and even given its own name: **The Dunning-Kruger effect** (2).

In her book *The Willpower Instinct* and the course based on it, McGonigal stresses the importance of self-knowledge and analysis of previous failures to design successful strategies for behavioural change.

I couldn't agree more.

We've discussed the importance of learning from your mistakes and previous attempts - successful or not. But analysing your failures can also help you prepare for temptations and prepare to fight them better in the future. Because, whether you believe it or not, temptations will happen.

The better you are prepared, the less impact temptations will have on your progress - not only by minimising the pitfalls, but also by helping you recover from setbacks.

Here are 5 strategies that I've found most helpful in fail-proofing my habit systems.

1. Plan It on a Bad Day

Since you've got this far in seeking a solution to your problem, you're not only aware of the problem, you're also - motivated. And now the trick is to match your tasks with the amount of motivation you have.

One of the best strategies to use your motivation for a change wisely is to plan that change on a bad day.

We commonly underestimate how much time and effort various projects will take. It's even worse when it comes to predicting our behaviour in the future.

The so-called **empathy gap** (3) is a cognitive bias that makes us underestimate the influence of visceral/strong emotional states on our behaviour in the future. So with your 'cold' head on, you may be thinking: 'Nah, I'd be alright with that diet. I'll just distract myself when I'm hungry,' minimising the power of feeling hungry, or craving that chocolate bar.

When you're all excited and rational, you're pumped with

motivation and inspiration, and you're thinking you can move mountains. And since you can move mountains, you should be able to move your two legs and the rest of your body and go for a run after work.

Well, after work you're tired, emotionally drained, frustrated with the long drive home, hungry, and you'd rather plant yourself in front of the TV than go out running in the rain.

And this is how your fabulous plan goes out of the window.

'It's really easy to agree to a diet, if you're not hungry,' writes Baumeister (4).

So my response to **the cold-hot empathy gap** is to plan the change on a bad day, or at least an average day. When you're not 'pumped with enthusiasm,' with your realistic, if not slightly pessimistic hat on, you will be planning for a day like that.

If you can make yourself work out on a bad/average day - imagine how much easier it will be on a day when you're brimming with energy and enthusiasm for your new workout routine?

2. Minimise Temptations

My top tip on fail-proofing your habit solution is to **eliminate or at least minimise the number of temptations** you're exposed to.

It's so much easier to eat healthier if you don't have unhealthy food in your fridge and cupboard.

It's so much easier to get on with your writing if you have no other tempting websites open in your browser.

I've got a sweet tooth, that's why I try not to bake, even though I love baking. I also try not to buy sweets.

My exercise routine is the quintessence of temptation minimisation. People are very surprised to hear I run regularly, even though running is one of my least favourite sports. But I can run whenever I like, including 6 am. I don't need a partner to run, like I would if I wanted to play one of my favourite sports - tennis. Since I run along my street or in the local park, I don't have to wait for anything to be open. I don't have to drive there, or park my car, or fight for my turn in the machine/room, in the swimming lane, or remember to take the pass to let me in.

You can laugh if you like, but hey - these are all legitimate excuses I used previously when trying to establish a regular exercise routine with activities I like much more than running. So once I'd identified my previous failures - what had tempted me off the chosen path - it was actually an easy choice.

Look at the previous attempts of achieving this specific goal or building this habit you're pursuing right now. Use the information in Part 3 to inform this step.

- What are the most common reasons you've defaulted on your new regime in the past?
- What can you do to eliminate it in the future?
- If you can't eliminate it, how can you reduce the likelihood of this happening again?

- How can you limit its influence or impact?

Be as realistic as you can, even slightly on the pessimistic side when assessing your ability to deal with temptations. Remember the cold-hot empathy gap described above and you'll thank yourself for your smart planning later.

3. Use If-Then Future Planning

The best way to deal with temptations is to eliminate/minimise them as much as possible. But sometimes it will not be possible, because life is life and you can't just cut out certain things completely.

For those moments of temptation you can't eliminate, use **If - Then planning.**

If - then planning is a form of implementation intention, which I covered in chapter 16.

What you do is plan ahead what you're going to do in those tricky moments when you're facing the habit-related decision.

To use this strategy to its full potential, you need to know when you are most likely to fail. Use previous experience as a guide: look for patterns in the way you failed at achieving the goal before. The explorations you did in Part 3, particularly chapter 12 will be helpful here.

In case of doubt, err on the side of caution. It's better to underestimate your ability to resist temptation and then be pleasantly surprised than the other way around. Of course, you won't be able to cover every possible obstacle, but at least look for patterns and cover your most common slip-ups.

Once you've got a list of the most common temptation scenarios, plan for what you're going to do if you encounter one of them.

For example, if you want to cut down on fast food, and you know you're most likely to eat it when you're working late, you may want to come up with the following plan:

- If I'm working late, then I will defrost and have one of the meals I batch-cooked.

This plan would entail developing a habit of batch-cooking regularly and freezing one-portion meals.

Or, if you're working towards a regular exercise regime and you know in the past, you've given your runs a miss on rainy days, you may want to come up with the following plan:

- If it's raining, then I will do a series of cardio exercises at home,' or '... I will go to the gym,' etc.

4. Introduce Extra Decision Points

Since my willpower is unimpressive by nature, I need to be quite devious when designing my systems so I can outsmart myself and continue on the chosen path.

I am a sad victim of an instant gratification monkey that lives in my brain, so beautifully described by Tim Urban in his excellent TEDTalk (5).

My life is a constant struggle to delay gratification, push on for another five minutes, and another five. Sometimes I wonder how I even got through university (all 6 years of it). And even if I don't always win, over the years I've developed a number of ways to deal with the monkey constantly demanding her share of Reward.

If you, like me, have failed many times, if you feel you can't rely on your willpower, then feel free to pick some of my tips.

Once you've eliminated as many temptation pitfalls as you can, and limited the impact of a few more with your smart planning, get prepared for those instances when a temptation to steer off the chosen track pops up and surprises you.

When faced with a temptation, the emotional side of us just wants to indulge, or default to the familiar old behaviour, and wants it NOW. While the rational side is trying to argue that if you don't do it, you'd be better off in the future. And very often the emotional side wins.

But you can give yourself enough time to cool down and get the rational self back into the driver's seat - slow yourself down and introduce extra decision points.

Extra decision points are barriers to not following on your new behaviour plan or pursuing what would otherwise be your old habit or undesired automatic behaviour. The aim of those extra barriers is to create time/space between you making your decision not to do what you were intending to do and actually actioning it.

Say you are trying to stop yourself checking your phone when you're working. Introducing an extra decision point would be wrapping your phone into a few layers of paper, sellotaping it, and locking it in a drawer (for hardcore phone addicts, you can also put the key on the highest shelf in the house that requires you climb a ladder and locking the ladder in the cellar, etc.).

If you decide you want to check your phone - you've got to go through all those steps to get to it - a lot of time to rethink your decision, and hopefully - return to the tasks you were supposed to be working on.

I've done a lot of locking/hiding away of sweets to make it harder for me to eat them. This was one of the strategies I implemented in my recent Marshmallow Experiment (6). It worked.

I also use it when I'm working on a project that takes time to complete. With my low threshold for boredom and inability to sit still for long, I face multiple temptations to just get up and walk away from my workspace on one errand or another. So what I do is - I 'chain myself to my desk'. Not literally, but the idea is the same.

I sit in a corner with a wall on one side, a window just behind me, a big table in front of me and block the only exit with another chair. Getting up and walking away from my workspace requires moving chairs and squeezing behind them, and getting tangled in the curtains - that's a few extra decision points to pause and rethink my actions. So unless I absolutely have to get up, I often change my mind and stay put, working away.

5. Accountability Strategies

Accountability is a very common strategy people use to stick to their goals, particularly when it comes to long-term goals such as weight loss and habit building. From accountability buddies to accountability coaches, to signing contracts and making bets.

Common sense tells us it's easier to achieve a long-term goal or a major behaviour change if we get others involved, whether as support and cheerleaders, or to accompany us on the journey.

Generally accepted wisdom is that making your resolutions public, even if it's only disclosing it to a friend, or close family members, helps us keep those commitments. It's the sense of social accountability, having someone expecting something of you, that is at work here. But new evidence suggests this may not necessarily be the case. Research (7, 8) shows people who publicly commit to achieving identity goals (goals that influence the sense of who they are, e.g., career-related goals, behaviours linked with parenting, etc.) are less likely to actually achieve those goals because just talking about their goal made them think they've achieved it.

Accountability works through two main mechanisms:

- Social support
- Loss aversion (9)

Social support

This is very important when it comes to working towards a behaviour change, or long-term goal. You not only want people around you to cheer you and support you on your journey, you need them to accept you are changing your habits, which directly or indirectly affects them as well. Social support is also a way to boost your motivation - it's that someone who turns up on a rainy day and says, 'Come on, put your rain jacket on and we'll go for that run/walk.' It's the friendly ear at the other end of the phone, listening to your struggles with your diet, etc.

However, the **loss aversion** side of social accountability is a bit more complicated. This is the main issue I have with an accountability approach to boosting your motivation. Many of the contract or bet-based 'commitment devices' work through loss aversion – the human tendency to avoid losses, even if you can potentially gain more. Commonly, services such as StickK make you commit to your goal and put your money or your reputation on the line if you don't achieve it. And yes, there is a lot of evidence that supports the use of loss aversion as a motivational strategy (10), but loss aversion is also an extrinsic motivator and as such - prone to lose its effectiveness.

Personally, I'm not a fan of commitment devices. I am in the 'keep it to yourself' camp, probably because I'm an introvert and consider this sort of stuff quite private. Also, I believe that I'm either in or not - committed or not. And if I'm committed, I'll find ways to make sure I deliver on the promise. Adding an extra layer of accountability usually just causes me extra stress by me pushing to have it done before the deadline or even to higher expectations. Sounds great, but most of the time it just removes the flexibility and is a source of stress. Loss aversion doesn't really work for me.

Having said that, accountability strategies work for many people, so don't dismiss it and check if it works for you. But, as with anything, don't push on if you find it ineffective.

Some common accountability strategies are:

- **Accountability buddy/group/coach** - a person or a group of people who you tell about your habit-based goal and ask to support you and hold you accountable. You can also simply set up a social media or a blog challenge and comment to report on your progress regularly. Even though you may not lose anything, this creates an expectation of you progressing towards your goal.
- **Commitment contracts, etc.** - services such as StickK, Gym-Pact, or Fatbet that operate on commitment contracts and loss avoidance (Gym-Pack even pays you for achieving your goals). You can also make your own 'pacts' with your nearest and dearest.

As with every other strategy and tactic, use it if it works for you and doesn't harm you, or anyone else.

Missed a Day?

'Focus on the journey, not the destination,' writes S.J. Scott, a habit expert, in his book *Bad Habits No More*. (11). Don't worry about the bigger picture, just keep going, day-by-day, keep practicing your new routine.

Research shows (12) that missing on a day in your habit routine does not make a difference to our habit formation process, but psychologically it may.

Don't worry when you happen to miss a day, but don't let yourself go for too long either.

Life gets in the way of the best laid plans, so accept that. Sometimes you will be just too busy or too tired, or maybe sick, or you may have something super-important to do. Don't beat yourself up about not 'turning up' one day. But get back on track as soon as possible. Don't let the 'not turning up' become a pattern.

When does it become a pattern? You may have your own individual definition of pattern, for me it goes like: once is happenstance, twice is a coincidence, three is a pattern.

The more days you miss, the harder it will be to return to your routine. This is why, yet again, starting small and 'turning up' to practice your new behaviour is what matters most. Also, have a plan for getting back on track and implement it.

Time to Take Action

Don't underestimate the power of temptations. Think of the ways you can be tempted off your path towards your new habit. Use your knowledge of yourself and your context, and your understanding of your previous successes and failures to inform your strategies for dealing with temptations.

Choose at least one strategy for preventing temptations and

at least one for dealing with temptations, and record them in your Workbook.

In this chapter I've given you strategies for minimising the frequency and impact of temptations to not follow your new Routine. Remember, although those strategies work for me, and many other people, you need to find those that work for you. The best way to find out? Try and test. Give it a good go, and if you feel this is not working, try another one. In my experience, I get the best results when I use more than one strategy, particularly in cases where I know I tend to struggle a lot.

Keep trying until you find something that helps you stick to your routine in a satisfactory way.

In the next chapter I'll show you how to deal with resistance, so you can get underway with your new Routine.

HACK YOUR **HABITS**

Chapter 19:
5 Ways to Kill Resistance Upfront

Many people find that the hardest part of getting into a Routine is to start it, get going.

Once you're underway, it's okay. But overcoming that initial resistance is very hard.

Whole books have been written about overcoming resistance and making that first step. Stephen Pressfield's *The War of Art* (1) is my favourite. Pressfield writes about fighting resistance to write and to doing whatever is needed to pursue our dreams.

> *'It's not the writing part that is hard.*
> *What's hard is sitting down to write.*
>
> *What's keeping us from sitting down is Resistance.'*

Being a writer myself, I agree with Pressfield.

You know what you need to do. You know why and for what you want to do it. All you need to do now - is get going, but you keep finding things to do instead.

Oh, procrastination...

Let's look at how to procrastination-proof your habit system.

Below is a list of various strategies and tactics that I've found helpful in eliminating procrastination/ resistance when establishing new habits and breaking old ones.

1. Address the Underlying Cause

There are multiple reasons why people procrastinate, including procrastinating on carrying out the desired behaviours. Whether it's going to the gym, cooking a healthy meal, or keeping your files in order - before the new behaviour becomes automatic, resistance keeps you watching TV, looking at 'one more little post' on social media, or skipping a healthy meal today and promising you will start from tomorrow.

Procrastination, as Pressfield writes (1) is the most common manifestation of resistance. It's sneaky, because it's not a complete denial or that you don't want to do it. It's not because you forgot you were going to do it. On the contrary: you procrastinate because you think about that new behaviour, and you still want to do it, but... not now - maybe tomorrow.

We all procrastinate for different reasons, so you may need to find out why you procrastinate on your new behaviour, even though you know why you should do it.

The most common reasons people procrastinate are:

- Fear of failure (or success)
- Feeling overwhelmed by the size of the task
- Not knowing what to do
- Having a knowledge or a skill gap
- Not having enough interest/motivation in the task

Since you've got to this point in searching for better ways of building good habits, we can safely assume you have enough interest and motivation in pursuing the desired behaviour.

So let's look at the other common reasons why you may procrastinate and find remedies to overcome them.

Fear of failure or success

If you're procrastinating because of the fear of failure or success - you may need to **work on it**. Dig deeper into the subconscious reasons why you feel like that. You may need to explore your **motivation for and against achieving your habit goal**. You may need to look into your **confidence** or **self-esteem**. It may be that you have some **competing goals** or **expectations** that you have not uncovered or addressed.

Unfortunately, exploring and addressing the underlying fear of failure of success is beyond the scope of this book. I recommend you consider talking to a trusted, appropriately trained professional, such as a psychotherapist, counsellor, or your family doctor if you feel this is hindering your personal growth.

Fear of failure or success is quite common among

creative types. Pressfield has his own, very interesting take on how to deal with it. He describes his strategies in *The War of Art* (1) and more extensively in *Turning Pro* (2). If you are a creative type - an aspiring writer, painter, musician - I recommend you read his books.

In a nutshell, he recommends that you should **treat your creative pursuits like a job and 'just turn up and get on with it.'** He also talks about not taking success or failure personally, seeking help when needed, self-validation, and many other strategies.

Feeling overwhelmed or not knowing what to do

I've grouped these two causes of procrastination together because they can be addressed with the same strategy.

If you feel overwhelmed by the size of the task or don't know where to start, what to do, break the task (your new Routine) into actionable steps and write it all down. I covered this in Chapter 16.

Having it clearly spelled out and easily available when needed can be very helpful when you're feeling lost.

For example, cooking a healthy meal can be an overwhelming task, particularly when you're just starting to cook healthily. Identify what you need to do and in what sequence and write it down. This may look like:

1. Grab a healthy cooking recipe book
2. Plan your meals for the week
3. Make the shopping list based on the recipes chosen
4. On the day - take out the recipe, etc.

Don't forget to always have your first step clearly identified, and make sure your steps are in logical order. This will help keep your focused on priorities at the given moment.

A knowledge or skill gap

This procrastination cause is a tricky one. If your new habit includes you using knowledge you don't yet have or are not confident in using (for example, knowing what healthy cooking includes), or requires you to use a skill you're not good at (such as an exercise routine that involves a type of exercise you're unfamiliar with) - it means that you have an extra barrier to overcome.

I'm not a fan of adding any more difficulty to an already difficult task of starting a new Routine or changing an old habit. My approach is very pragmatic: the easier your new Routine is, the easier it will be to get it embedded into your life.

However, sometimes there are situations when you will need to learn something new in order to implement your new behaviour - healthy cooking is a good example.

Again: make it as easy as you can, by preparing as much up front as possible. Learn whatever you can and get all the tools, gear, and ingredients ready before you start. To use the healthy cooking as an example, if you need to learn how to cook healthily - get a healthy cooking book, or read about it. Get some recipes and keep them handy, get all the necessary utensils and ingredients and keep them handy.

Keep reminding yourself that your goal is to create a healthy eating/cooking habit, not to become a healthy cooking master chef. Focus on practice, not performance - show up and keep doing, however badly or well you are able to perform at this stage. Mastery will follow.

2. Skip the First Step

If making that first step is the biggest challenge for you, address it by... skipping it. This is another strategy I like. It may sound funny, but it works.

This is how many companies make us avid collectors of their loyalty points - by giving us a few up-front, to 'get you started.' My daughter was given a 'thumb up' stamp on her brand new swimming card at the local YMHA on Day 1, even though she hadn't done any swimming yet. The only coffee shop where I ever bothered to get a 'frequent customer card' also offered me a card with the first stamp already on.

This strategy is called the Illusion of Progress (3) and it has been used in sales for a while, often in customer retention and loyalty programs. It's been proven to make people stick with the program for longer, persist in their efforts to 'collect the stamps' (and keep consuming/buying), keep going, and accelerate towards the goal as they can see it approaching (4). It's really simple - you still need to buy x number of coffees to get the free one, but with the first stamp already there, you feel you're closer to your goal.

Yes, it's a trick of the mind, but it's effective.

Chip and Dan Heath call this 'shrink the change' (5), and they go deeper into strategies for making the change feel smaller and less threatening than originally, but my favourite aspect of this approach is that it helps overcome the initial resistance.

Because we fall for this illusion. You've already got 2 stamps on your coffee card - only 8 more until your free coffee.

You've got to this chapter - chapter 19 - see, you're already underway.

I use this strategy to deal with resistance in my exercise routine (I put my running gear on first thing in the morning), as well as for avoiding procrastination on large, long-term projects (prepare my workstation the night before, often starting working on the task the night before, even if it's just writing a couple of lines).

If you want to exercise in the morning - put on your workout clothes, shoes included, straight after you get out of bed. More - sleep in your workout clothes. You've skipped the first step of having to put your gear on.

If you want to always work on your most challenging stuff before your family gets up, skip the first step and prepare your workspace in the evening to work on exactly that: have all the stuff you need ready for you, and nothing else.

3. The Path of Least Resistance

We've known that for years: when faced with a choice in getting to a goal, people (and animals, too) will follow **the path of least resistance or least effort** (6).

This approach is often poo-pooed by motivational gurus and inspirational speakers, who convey the message that we should be acting on higher-octane fuel and reaching for the stars.

Don't get me wrong, I'm not saying being aspirational is wrong. By all means, have a noble goal, a mission, follow your passion, extend your horizons and your comfort zone.

But if you just want to be able to get stuff done - **embrace the path of least resistance.**

The path of least resistance has been proven as a very effective strategy in getting people to save for retirement (7) or supporting decision-making in various settings (8).

Want to be able to exercise regularly? Decide on the type of exercise, time and day, place, and gear that **you are most likely to adhere to.**

Want to start cooking healthy meals? **Find the easiest way to do it** - with the gear you have access to, ingredients you can easily get, time and effort investment you can easily accommodate.

My exercise routine is the pinnacle of the path of least resistance. I've written about it earlier in this book, but let me take you through the steps that led to the decision to run 3 times a week, in the morning.

Exercise type: I needed something that did not require

driving (hate driving and parking), could be done whenever I'm ready (no 'opening hours'), without relying on other people, and without anyone getting in my way.

Time: best done on the days I need to wash my hair, so 3-4 times/week.

Best time of day: when I'm not tired, with some flexibility; not requiring much 'setup' time and 'wind down' time afterward.

My favourite sports are swimming and tennis and then rowing.

As you can see, the first two require getting to special places where I could practice it and those places are often open in certain hours only. Tennis usually involves finding a partner. Both carry a risk of other people 'getting in the way.'

Rowing could be done on a rowing machine in the garage, but it's an investment I wasn't able to make. Going to the gym to use their rowing machines - ticks all the wrong boxes, just like swimming and tennis.

Swimming is the worst, actually - with long setup and wind-down time (getting changed and showered before and after).

As I don't consider walking as exercise (I walk a lot, so I don't even notice it as exercise), you can see that running looks just perfect here.

Shifting my workout time from evenings, when I was prone to feeling tired or generally too overwhelmed to go out and run, to mornings (which is my favourite time of day) but carefully placing it at around 6 am- so the streets are still empty and I have enough time to shower and get ready for work afterwards, without impinging on the most productive time of day - was crucial to continuing with the regime.

The path of least resistance at its best.

Sometimes your path of least resistance may take you through steps that are not good for you, or somehow undermine the process of habit creation. Use it with caution and always exercise your own judgement.

Ultimately, it's your decision. I'm of the view that a system that performs in a predictable and reliable way and delivers a predictable and reliable outcome, even if the outcome is modest or of low quality, may be way better than delivering astonishing quality outcomes in an unpredictable and unreliable way, 'on the whim,' a.k.a. 'When inspiration strikes me.' Habits are about performing your behaviour regularly, so I don't really care about the quality of the outcome, at least not initially.

But as usual, exercise your own judgement.

4. The Default Option

A variation of the path of least resistance is **making your new routine the default option.**

This is a strategy where your desired behaviour becomes the only or the easiest available option to choose.

This technique originates from behavioural economics and is one of the strategies used in **choice architecture** (9). This particular strategy has generated a lot of debate not only because of potential ethical dilemmas (10), but also because of its effectiveness when it comes to getting people to become organ donors (11), saving for retirement (7), eating healthier (12).

The **default option is one of the most powerful willpower-boosting strategies**. The secret is to design your habit in a way that what you want to do is the easiest and most obvious thing to do. It's the ultimate version of eliminating temptations and embracing the path of least resistance. If you can make your desired behaviour the only choice you have, I believe you're onto a winner.

You can achieve it by combining a number of strategies, for example minimising/eliminating temptations, skipping the first step, and embracing the path of least resistance.

This is exactly what I've done multiple times in my life to make sure I walked to work: no easy access to car/hate driving, no monthly bus pass (spend the money on something else up front), don't know the timetable, walk on the other side of the road from the bus stops you'd need, or take a different route altogether.

To a large extent my current exercise routine is the default option. With my first step skipped (I'm already wearing my smelly workout clothes), I have to take a shower before I change into my regular clothes (and wash my hair), so I have no other option than to go out, tick off the 30-something minutes of running up and down the local hills before I can get my 'real day' underway.

If you want to consider The Default Option as your habit-building strategy: look for ways in which you can 'nudge' yourself to the right choice by leaving no other choices.

A word on the ethical aspects of this 'choice architecture'

This strategy is often criticised as being paternalistic or manipulating people. Here is my view: since this is a decision I'm making with my full informed consent, I know what I am getting into. This is a proven and fully informed deal I'm making with myself. So, again, as long as I don't harm myself or anyone else, or don't do anything illegal - I'm fine with it.

5. Make Your Habits Stupid Small

This is a strategy I've borrowed from Stephen Guise and his Mini Habits philosophy (13).

Stephen developed a whole philosophy around the idea of starting so small you can't say no. He has built multiple habits successfully and helped many other people achieve successful behavioural change using this very strategy.

It all started with one push-up a day.

He recommends that you choose your daily requirement for your positive behaviour as low as you can go and remain at that level. The trick is that this 'laughable' goal needs to be completed on daily basis, and you're free to do more. You don't have to, but you can. If you can meet the tiny requirement for the day, you've achieved success for the day.

Once again, it emphasises the effectiveness of focusing on practice rather than performance. You can read more about his strategy in the next chapter.

Whichever strategy you use, again, make sure it works for you, Experiment with different approaches, mix and match, including the techniques described in the previous chapter for increased effect.

Time to Take Action

Depending on your own procrastination patterns, choose at least one strategy to deal with resistance/procrastination and record it in your Workbook.

HACK YOUR **HABITS**

CHAPTER 20:
Guest Expert Chapter – Stephen Guise - Mini-Habits Strategy for Personal Development

Stephen Guise is a habit expert and a bestselling author. His book: 'Mini Habits. Smaller Habits. Bigger Results.' and his posts have helped hundreds of thousands of people transform their lives with a smart strategy of Mini Habits. I love his approach because it doesn't rely on flimsy motivation and it's super-effective against resistance. It helped me develop a regular back exercise routine, when I needed it badly.

It all started with One-Push-Up-Challenge...

'It's not what we do once in a while that shapes our lives. It's what we do consistently.' ~Anthony Robbins

I had experimented with personal development strategies for a decade. When I accidentally started my first mini habit— and the changes I made were actually lasting— I realized the prior strategies I relied upon were complete failures.

After years of experiments I can confidently tell you that Mini Habits is the greatest personal development strategy ever.

Yeah, it's a bold claim, but it's true.

Why Most Self-Development Strategies Fail

Your strategies determine whether you experience success or failure, whether you win or lose, and whether you get real results or continue wishing for them.

Most people don't know or understand the basic strategy equation:

Strategy's Success Rate = Effectiveness × Implementability

The world overemphasizes effectiveness over implementability so much we're typically blinded to the other part.

Yes, it makes sense to consider *if you can do something* before you focus on how effective it will be, but we often forget about it. When setting goals, people often don't take into account that their motivation and energy levels are going to fluctuate dramatically, and that will affect their ability to take actions. They'll assume their current state of mind and energy can be preserved or reactivated when the time comes to act. What ensues is a losing struggle against a brain that doesn't want to change (in that way).

Multiple studies show we chronically overestimate our abilities, willpower, and self-control (1). Once you recognize and adjust to this, brace yourself, because your life will rapidly change for the better.

So how can you fix it?

1. Make the Most of the Strategy Equation

Remember the basic strategy equation?

$$\textit{Strategy's Success Rate} = \textit{Effectiveness} \times \textit{Implementability}$$

The value of a strategy is a function of how effective it is and how well (or if) it can be implemented. Simply put: *does it work and can it be done?*

If your goal is to move an elephant onto a spot one mile away, you could play a song for the elephant to make it move. This strategy has 100% implementability (it's easy to do), but its effectiveness is really 0%. Though the elephant might move (if your song is *that* bad), there's no chance it would move to the right place.

When you multiply 100% x 0%, you get 0% - the strategy is worthless for accomplishing the goal.

Or, you could **carry the elephant on your back to the spot.** This strategy has 100% effectiveness (you'll get the elephant where you want it to be), but there is a little problem: elephants are far too big for humans to carry them, so the implementability of this strategy is 0%.

When you calculate the strategy's success rate, you get 0% again. If you could do it, it would work, but you can't do it.

2. A Strategy Will Never Work If the Action Has No Effect on the Goal or If the Action Is Impossible to Do

Obviously, nobody would even consider carrying an elephant on their back or playing a song to move it a mile away. It becomes less obvious when strategies have *mixed* scores of effectiveness and implementability.

We don't always consider the full equation (or we think we do, but our calculations are off).

I wanted to exercise consistently. The first strategy I tried was the default strategy of mankind—aim high and get motivated.

Aim high and get motivated effectiveness: 94%

We're talking about extreme exercise here. Let's get ripped in 90 days with P90X, okay? Or I could plan to exercise for 2 hours every day. Could you imagine how jacked I'd be if I did that? Nice. With an effectiveness score of 94%, this is looking attractive and motivating.

Aim high and get motivated implementability: 14%

Here's what happened: When I tried to do P90X (a 90-day program), I only did it for 30 days, and skipped some of *those* days.

When I tried to go to the gym consistently, I typically only made it for 2 weeks before quitting. I wanted that 94% effectiveness so much, but I struggled for *10 years* with horrid implementability. I figured it was my fault for not wanting it enough because I didn't understand the fundamental equation of strategy.

Aim high and get motivated total strategy success rate = 94% effectiveness x 14% implementability = 13.2% success rate

Ouch. That makes sense. In those 10 years, I didn't get far. And while I'm estimating these numbers, 13.2% success is awfully close to what studies have shown for typical goal achievement.

In my upcoming book, *Mini Habits for Weight Loss*, I discuss the success rate of people trying to lose weight. One study found after one year, 20% of people kept off 10% weight loss (longer term, that success rate drops) (2). Another study found that all resolutions have about a 19% success rate after two years, regardless of the goal (3). Both of these are likely higher than the actual, real world success rate.

3. Use The Mini-Habits Strategy

In late 2012, I started a fitness mini-habit. I began aiming for one push-up per day (4), using The Mini-Habits Strategy.

The Mini-Habits Strategy is forcing yourself to take 1-4 'stupid small' strategic actions every day. These actions are too small to fail, and too small to skip for special occasions. They serve dual purposes— to spark you to do more, and to become (mini) habits.

One push-up effectiveness: 42%

I'm not delusional. I know that doing one push-up won't bring the same results as an extreme workout, but it will bring greater short-term results than expected. On several occasions, my one push-up grew to full workouts. Thus, I think 42% effectiveness is fair.

One push-up implementability: 99%

Nothing is 100% implementable, because you could always choose not to do it or forget about it, even if it's as easy as one push-up. Regardless, a mini habit is as implementable as it gets. While society focuses on effectiveness, a mini-habit is focused on maximizing implementability.

One push-up total strategy success rate = 42% x 99% = 41.6% success rate

Though it easily surpasses the first strategy, 41.6% seems a bit low for a supposed superstar strategy. It surely seems way too low to me because I changed my life with this strategy in multiple areas. My one push-up became a full-time gym habit that rivaled the extreme workouts I targeted early on.

How come?

I forgot to calculate **the bonus modifiers**. A mini-habit is special because of its **superior implementability**. With 99% implementability, remarkable consistency is not only possible, but probable. This means habit formation and its associated decreased resistance will come. The real formula for a strategy's success rate isn't as simple as I first suggested.

Strategy's Success Rate = Effectiveness x Implementability (If Implementability > 90, Add Habit + Overachievement + Behavior Upgrade Bonuses)

Let's sum it all up then:

One Push-up Implementability: 99% (+ 60% Habit Bonus + 20% Overachievement Bonus + 40% Behavior Upgrade Bonus) = 219% Modified Implementability Score

One Push-up TRUE Strategy Success Rate = 42% x 219% = 92% Success Rate

From feedback I've received, 92% more closely mirrors the success rate and superior results of people who try mini-habits. The formula is laid out this way to show you why it's difficult to see the true success rate of different strategies.

Why Mini-Habits Strategy Works

1. Consistency by design

The first reason why Mini-Habits is the greatest personal development strategy ever is because it leverages the power of consistency by design. When something sounds 'stupid small,' your brain sees it as nonthreatening:

One push-up a day? You're joking.

Get rid of one possession every day? Worthless.

This gives people a much higher rate of success for reaching their goals.

2. No 'wasted motivation'

As if the superior success rate weren't enough, there's more to love about the mini-habits method.

The major fault people see in such a strategy is the concept of 'wasted motivation' - the idea that you don't take advantage of your true potential. On a day that you're able to do 150 push-ups, why would you aim for only one? If you only did one, that would waste all of your potential to do more. With a mini-habit, however, you will never be held back.

With Mini-Habits Strategy you can always do more if you feel like it with 'bonus reps'. Since our motivation fluctuates daily, the mini-habits model allows us to maximize whatever amount of motivation we have. It isn't based on reaching a goal, it's based on the reality of each day. Mini-Habits Strategy adapts to you on a daily basis.

3. Mini-Habits (ironically) supercharge your motivation

With the freedom to do how much you want after your minimal requirement, you'll feel in control (autonomy). By seeing the impact of daily action, you see the real results that can compound and you'll begin to believe that your choices and actions can really make a difference in your life. All of this serves to supercharge your motivation.

4. You don't have to fight resistance

Mini-Habits help you win the willpower game.

If you're resisting your single push-up today— try getting in push-up position, or easier, lie on your stomach on the floor. If your mini-habit is to drink one glass of water every day, you can make it smaller by deciding to fill a glass with water, or one step further, pick up a glass. If your mini-habit is writing 50 words a day and you're resisting, open up your word processor and write one word. My rule of thumb is to minify my desired habit until it sounds stupid and you don't feel resistance any more.

You won't need to do this most of the time as your mini-habits are already 'stupid small,' but remember you have this in your arsenal for times of extreme resistance. Too small does not exist in regards to mini-habits. If you're unsure, go with the smaller option. For ideas of mini-habits to implement, visit www.minihabits.com.

This is **the key of the Mini-Habits system**. You're going to repeat this too-small-to-fail action every day. Just as important as making your mini-habit small is making your thoughts small too. You must embrace this mini-requirement as if it is a full goal. This means if you meet the tiny requirement, you're successful for the day. If you can do that, you will get the 'big' results you desire.

By combining world class consistency with opportunistic overachievement for short- and long-term progress, mini-habits is the world's greatest strategy for personal growth.

Stephen Guise

Read more in 'Why Mini-Habits is the Greatest Personal Development Strategy Ever' (5) and Mini Habits. Smaller Habits. Bigger Results (6)

CHAPTER 21:
Test, Track, Tweak, and Celebrate Your Progress

Congratulations, you've built your very own habit system on autopilot. Well done.

But before you start telling everyone about it, let's just check if everything is working.

I'm a big fan of testing strategies I use. And the best way to do it is to put it to work and track the progress.

In order to know if it's working you need to be clear on your definition of success - what do you expect the system to do?

While outcome-oriented goal tracking of the progress focuses on the journey towards the goal: how many words you've written, how many kilograms or centimetres you've lost, exams passed, etc., habit-based goals are about practice rather than performance. Because of that, progress tracking should reflect the performance - the 'turning up.'

How to Track Progress Toward Your Habit Goal

My suggestion is that you pick a tracking method that **makes sense** to you in **the context of the habit** you're pursuing and is **aligned with your overall motivation** for the habit, and your main motivational driver. This way you're not only tracking progress, but also reinforcing motivation for continuing with the new routine.

A tracking method that make sense is one that reports on your progress toward your goal. Sounds obvious, but some people can get mixed up here. Let's just go back to the difference between habit-based and outcome-oriented goal.

When you're working towards an outcome-oriented goals, such as weight loss, fitness level, improved productivity - you will be choosing and tracking some metrics that matter to you, e.g. kilograms lost, your running speed or number of reps made, or how many words you've written today.

But habit-based goals are different. With **habit-based goals** you need to **focus on practice, not performance.** So your task is to find a way to **mark the completion of your routine.**

A simple 'tick' on the calendar is the most common strategy to track your progress in habit-building. There are other, similar strategies that are effective, too, such as keeping a tally of your exercise sessions, or putting a paperclip into a jar every time you make a sales call. Tim Dyrsmid, a stockbroker, created a powerful habit of making 120 phone calls to his customers every day, and as a result, not only quickly becoming a top performer at his company, but also helping them make a lot of money. His strategy is often called 'the paper clip jar strategy,' and it relies on shifting paperclips from one jar to another as you complete your daily actions (1).

One of the most popular strategies for keeping track of your habit progress, which has become a habit-forming strategy, is 'don't break the chain' or 'Seinfeld strategy' (2). Seinfeld's (a famous comedian) strategy for being a better comic was to create better jokes, and the way to create better jokes was to write them every day. He would put a cross (x) with a big red marker on the calendar every day he did his share of joke writing. The crosses would create a chain and the task was to keep that chain growing without any breaks.

Having a visual way to track your progress can be very powerful, because you immediately know if you've done what you were supposed to do or not. This was what helped.

Align Your Tracking System with Your Overall Motivation

A well-chosen tracking metric not only gives you feedback on how you're progressing towards your habit goal, but also taps into the power of your motivational fuel.

However, if you choose a tracking method that does not align with your overall motivation (intrinsic or extrinsic), you may struggle to keep going.

A word of warning: because of the way tracking works, I feel the traditional way of tracking progress is heavily biased towards people driven by mastery. Ticking off days or moving the paperclips reflects how well you've mastered the Routine you're working towards, how much your performance improved, etc. In my opinion, this makes tracking harder for others who don't care so much about mastery.

If you're driven by **mastery**, let your monitoring system reflect it by, for example, creating a progress chart tracking your progress to mastery of your habit. This can be reflected in what you call your tracking system or the indicator you're tracking. For instance, you may want to track 'one day closer to being fit,' or 'one day closer to mastering my time.'

For those of you fuelled by **autonomy**, track your progress to autonomy. Think of your tracking exercise in terms of how it brings you closer to your dream of independence/freedom. To use the example above: 'one day closer to my own business' (when developing a productivity routine), or 'one day closer to early retirement' (saving habit), 'being in control of my health' (healthy eating habits), etc. Assuming that you focusing on practice, not performance, you can also note how much you've managed to save today, or what you were able to do independently that you could not before (I could walk 2 flights of stairs without getting short of breath).

And for those **purpose-driven,** make sure your monitoring system is linked to what you care about - how many people you've helped, how many messages you received from your students about the impact you've made, etc.

Tweaking the System

The point of testing your system is obviously to ensure it delivers on the promise.

Keep your Habit Goal clearly in mind when testing. Remember to focus on **practice, not performance, and have a schedule, not a deadline**.

My running routine is about doing over 30 minutes of exercise 3 times per week. And this is what I do. For years I tried to train to run a half marathon, but I must admit - I find running so boring I've never been able to exceed 65 minutes of running, even when listening to podcasts, music, or audiobooks. So, after multiple failed attempts resulting in me having to restart the whole running adventure from the beginning (because I would inevitably have a too-long break) I decided to focus on the habit of running and practice.

And my new system is indeed delivering on the promise - I've been running without any major break for 16 months at the time of writing.

So test if your system is delivering on the goal of making you perform the new behaviour every time you are supposed to do so. If you want to get up earlier every day - is your system making you get up every day at the set time? If you want to cook healthier - is your system making you do it every day, etc.

If your system is not delivering

If you feel your system is not delivering, identify what's not working and tweak it.

Having a better understanding which element of the system is not working helps you tweak it. Again, it's all about targeting what's not working instead of shooting in the dark.

- If you are not performing your routine as scheduled **because you forget about it**, it's likely that your Cue is not effective. Find another Cue and experiment with it. Follow the principles described in Chapter 13.
- If you notice you remember when and what you were supposed to do, but **don't feel compelled enough** to carry out your new behaviour, you may need to look at the underlying reasons for that and address them.

Most common reasons for habit system failure

1. **The cost of implementing the new behaviour versus continuing with the old habit is too high** - consider lowering the cost by:
   - Addressing resistance (see Chapter 19 for tips)
   - Dealing with temptations (see Chapter 18 for tips)
   - Experimenting with another Reward (see Chapter 15 for suggestions)

As this is the least costly exercise, I'd suggest if you're not sure of the underlying problem, start here.

However, if you have done everything you could and your system is still not delivering, I suspect a deeper problem may be at work here. Look below for suggestions on how to tackle it.

2. **You are pursuing the wrong goal** - This is a biggie, but it can happen.

Whether you got something wrong in the initial process of goal-identification, or your life situation changed along the way - Go through the realistic and achievable desired outcome exercise described in Chapter 9.

If your life circumstances changed substantially, have a look at Chapter 25 for tips on how to tackle it.

3. **You are pursuing your goal at the wrong time, in the wrong context, etc.**

If you really want to achieve that habit goal, but your environment - external, or internal, or social - is just going against you, throwing physical illness, financial stress, relationship breakups, physical limitations at you, it may be that you need to consider re-prioritising your goals.

Remember that the more goals you are chasing, the less likely you are to achieve them. Are you really ready for this massive change in your cooking and shopping habits? Can you afford going to the gym every other day with the new baby in tow?

Go through the steps described earlier in the book and be honest with yourself. Also be kind to yourself. If the time is wrong, the time is wrong, and going against the tide may cost you more than the returns achieved from achieving the goal.

Celebrate Your Success

Obvious, isn't it?

Well, yes, but - wait, there is more.

By all means, celebrate your successes - if that helps keep you going on that long journey. But be mindful this can be a double-edge sword.

Do you know when people are most likely to indulge in eating comfort foods? You may be surprised to learn that 86% of surveyed Americans (3) are likely to seek comfort foods when they're happy, and 74% when they celebrate or to reward themselves.

Yes, indulging in unwanted behaviours as a way of rewarding yourself for success can jeopardise your future progress. I have experienced it myself.

I recently realised one of the biggest willpower challenges I face is 'because I deserve a break/something nice, etc.' This has jeopardised my diet many, many times, but also slowed my progress towards other goals. I'm working very hard on overcoming this tendency.

Celebrate your success, by all means, but be mindful of what you do, how much, and make sure you don't slip off your path towards your chosen habit.

Time to Take Action

Taking into consideration your main motivational driver, as well as the outcome you're seeking with this particular habit, come up with a way of tracking your progress towards your habit goal. Don't forget that you need **practice, not performance and have a schedule, not a deadline.**

Write your strategy for tracking your progress in the Workbook.

Hopefully, you've got your system set up and tested. Yay. It's running like a dream. Congratulations and well done, yet again.

Now, go and celebrate – moderately and without undermining the effort you have put into getting to this point.

Next, we'll look at the most common issues that people face when maintaining good habits.

HACK YOUR **HABITS**

Part 6:

TACKLE COMMON BARRIERS TO HABIT FORMATION

- Chapter 22: 6 Steps to Discover What Motivates You
- Chapter 23: Dealing with Willpower Shortages and Outages
- Chapter 24: Guest Experts Chapter - Martin Meadows: 5 Unusual but Effective Strategies to Build Willpower
- Chapter 25: What to Do When Life Gets in the Way
- Chapter 26: Help. My Support System Isn't Very Supportive.
- Chapter 27: 'What the Hell' Effect and Getting Back On Track

HACK YOUR **HABITS**

Chapter 22:
6 Steps to Discovering What Motivates You

As I said earlier, *'If you match your goal to your motivation, it not only means you will be fuelling your journey with what really drives you in life, but also - it means you will be setting yourself goals that take into consideration how much motivation you have.'*

Motivation is the fuel that powers your vehicle - the clearer you are what you need to put in the tank, the more likely you are to get to your destination. So, before you embark on that journey towards a healthier, more productive, happier you, you'd better make sure you know what type of fuel you need to put in your motivational tank.

Finding out what motivates you, not only to develop the specific habit you're working on, but generally in life - is key to successful transformation of your habits.

Human motivation is a complex area that has been explored for years. Some theories are better supported by evidence than others. This is a simplified take on human motivation, and one that focuses on theories better known to general public- **Maslow's hierarchy of needs** (1) and **self-determination theory** (2). If you're interested in exploring this in more detail, check the references section.

First of all, let's be clear - from the point of view of hierarchy of needs, it's hard to talk about higher level needs, such as self-esteem or self-actualisation (this is where most self-improvement goals originate), if your basic needs aren't met. If you've ever experienced stress, uncertainty of unmet needs related to a safe roof over your head, food on the table, or a serious health condition, you likely experienced that your motivation was driven by money or any other means that enabled you to have those basic needs met. And that's totally normal.

So to truly be able to access higher-level motivators, you need to have your basic physiological, safety, and to some extent, love and belonging needs met.

And once we get to the point of a sense of belonging, self-esteem, and particularly actualisation, we enter a realm of self-improvement. That's why, when discussing anything motivation related, I think in terms of self-actualisation, or self-determination.

Let's take a look at how motivation works.

How Motivation Works

From the psychological point of view, motivation can either come from within (**intrinsic motivation**), or be driven by external factors (**extrinsic motivation**).

Extrinsic motivation boils down to two elements: **rewards**

and punishment. It relies on the simple principle that most humans (like animals) respond positively to rewards by doing more of the behaviour that is reinforced, and avoid behaviours that provoke punishment. Interestingly, while we tend to think about extrinsic reward in terms of 'carrots and sticks', these drivers are important to help children feel secure and cared for by parents, school establishments, (think rules and regulations, etc.). Internalisation of extrinsic motivation is linked to competence as well.

Most typical extrinsic motivators are:

- **Rewards**: money and its equivalents (such as coupons, gift cards, work perks, badges, titles, etc.), non-monetary material goods (gifts, food, etc.), praise, acceptance, reputation, privileges, promotions
- **Punishment:** naming & shaming, pain (physical or emotional), rejection, social ostracism, exclusion from a group, fines, loss of material or goods or privileges

As you can see, this is a wide collection of drivers that can have powerful effects on our behaviour as children and adults.

However, the effects of extrinsic motivation often wear off with time and use (3). As far as my motivational drivers are concerned, at some point, no matter how much more you want to pay me, if I am not interested in the task, I am not likely to do it. And if you threaten me with some sort of punishment, say, a loss of reputation or money, it may give me a bit more of a push, but still, overall, there is a limit to how far this type of motivation can drive me.

Extrinsic motivation can work quite well, but its appeal usually wears off in time, or when you run out of rewards to collect.

Intrinsic motivation is much more powerful and lasting. It fuels people to pursue their goals over a number of years, even entire lifespans. It is driven by passion, internal fire, and deepest human desires to achieve mastery, personal fulfilment, and autonomy. These are all big words, powerful concepts, and definitely from the top of the Maslow's hierarchy of needs pyramid.

Intrinsic motivation is often broken down into a few main drivers. The Self-Determination theory (4) often refers to the following three main intrinsic motivators: the needs of **competence, autonomy, and relatedness.**

Personally, I prefer Daniel Pink's take on it (5) with the distinction of: **autonomy, mastery** (competence), and **purpose**.

Mastery is about **self-improvement**, the urge to improve and develop yourself, your skills, your knowledge.

Autonomy is the **desire to direct your own life**, be the master of your destiny and your own boss.

Purpose is about the **need to do things** for reasons other and **bigger than yourself**; helping others, building a better world.

I prefer this distinction, because I believe purpose is a broader concept. It encompasses relatedness to some extent, but takes it even further - to working for a bigger goal that extends beyond just your own immediate environment, to following your passion of serving others, working on things that have potential to transform the world.

I also like Pink's approach to explaining intrinsic drivers because it can be directly applied to how many people choose to live and work these days. We see it quite often with successful people - entrepreneurs, big leaders, many celebrities, as well as many so-called 'everyday people.'

Intrinsic motivation is much more powerful, as it has the potential to fuel us throughout our lives. It makes us move mountains and undertake long-term projects that may not bring results for many years. However, there is also a downside to intrinsic motivation - being the big and powerful force, it sometimes fails us in day-to-day, dull-as-hell situations.

How to Use Intrinsic and Extrinsic Motivation

So, you may ask, which one is better for habit formation - intrinsic or extrinsic motivation?

Both are useful if used smartly.

The most effective rewards are a combination of intrinsic and extrinsic motivators. Yes - in order for your motivation to work well for you, in any area of life, and particularly in personal development and self-improvement, in the short and long run, you need a good mixture of both intrinsic and extrinsic motivators. You need a powerful long-lasting intrinsic motivator to guide you and some short-term extrinsic strategies you can use for the day-to-day struggles.

This is where most self-improvement goals fail: in the brutal reality of trying to implement lasting changes on a day-to-day basis, particularly when things aren't going smoothly, workloads pile up and stress levels are through the roof.

Reminding yourself of your aspirations to become a better version of yourself, going back to your values, your mission and purpose can be helpful, but **a material reward** may have a **faster and more powerful effect** on the spot. Just think about all those times when the only thing that helped you survive those hectic days at the office, or boring meetings filled with conflict, was the thought of a nice hot bath and a glass of wine (bar of chocolate).

While intrinsic drivers work best for long-term projects, such as building habits, **extrinsic rewards get you through hard days**, particularly if you feel there is nothing left in the tank and you still need to continue with the routine.

The exact strategies you can use in the reward process of habit formation are described in chapter 15.

Don't Work for Motivation - Make it Work for You

Have you ever felt inspired by other people's pursuits? I have. And I've met many people who fell for other people's dreams.

I've had a friend, Betsy, who, inspired by her parents- both in healthcare careers, decided to become a nurse to help people. In nursing school, she was a good student, eager to learn. Her teachers were always full of praise for her. But as she progressed, she felt less and less happy. But she kept pushing on, because everyone around her - her patients, colleagues, teachers were telling her she would make a fantastic nurse. But at the bottom of her heart, she wasn't happy. Despite overwhelming evidence that her work was doing a lot of good for others, she was feeling unfulfilled.

She hit a really low point shortly after graduation. Initially she thought it was just stress and hard work she put into completing her qualifications, so she took time off to reflect on what had been happening with her. This was when she discovered she missed the ability to make her own decision, she was just following orders. She did not have much time for her creative pursuits either. She realised that autonomy, independence, and creativity were some of the things she valued most in her life, but they had been unfulfilled. No wonder her soul felt empty and starving.

'It was a very strange, but incredibly liberating discovery,' Betsy said. 'I became inspired by my parents' great work and their passion for helping others. And I still want to help others, but first of all - I need to make sure I'm happy and fulfilled.' At the time of writing, she had quit her nursing career and was supporting herself fully from her craft business. She is a much happier person now.

'Successful people set goals congruent with their personality, their values, interests, strengths, skills, mission and purpose,' writes Chris Friesen, a psychologist experienced in helping athletes, entrepreneurs, and professionals achieve their top performance (6).

You've heard that so many times - we only have one life, so

why wasting it on pursuing the goals that don't really feed your soul?

But I warn you against pursuing goals and dreams that are not really aligned with who you are, no matter how inspirational and good they sound. **If it doesn't feed your soul, it doesn't feed your soul**. Regardless of how big the reward you're getting is, if you don't care about it - you will feel unrewarded and deprived.

You will crash and burn.

Discover What Motivates You and Use it Wisely

I don't know about you, but discovering how motivation works was an eye-opener and the beginning of a new era for me. It was a painful discovery, but as liberating as Betsy's. Without having the words to describe it, I always felt I needed to constantly learn and feel I was improving - my knowledge, my skills, my abilities. But for many years, I tried to be like other people - to follow passions other people suggested I might have. My parents insisted on seeking financial stability, job security, and social conformity. Many of my friends at the time had inspiring visions of saving people's lives, or making money and seeking power.

I tried to fit in, while still trying to feed my soul. And while initially my academic and then clinical training pursuits provided me with multiple opportunities for learning and improvement, after I finally passed all my exams and became a specialist psychiatrist ('board certified', 'college fellow', or consultant psychiatrist), I started running out of avenues to explore. Yes, clinical knowledge is constantly expanding, but it's often just reiterations of stuff we already know. Not challenging enough for me to feel I'm really evolving. So I continued telling myself lies about what drove me in life.

A couple of years ago I got to the point where I realised I could not progress any further without a significant change in career trajectory. Since I did not want to go into research, work for pharmaceutical companies, or do more healthcare management, I decided to quit medicine completely and focus on other things. I've set up my own business, got involved in a number of technology start-ups, trained as a teacher of ESOL (English for Speakers of Other Languages). And most of all - I finally got seriously into writing.

I am a much happier person now. My soul is slowly recovering from years of starvation and living incongruent with my values.

All that because I had the courage to be honest with myself and uncover my most powerful motivational driver in life, and follow it.

How to Identify What Motivates You

Okay, enough theory, let's look at some practical exercises to help you discover what motivates you in life, so that you can exploit it in your journey to better habits.

Answer these questions with as much courage as you can. No

one needs to hear it - it's an internal and very personal exploration. You can write it down, or not. You can write it down and then destroy it completely, or frame it and put it proudly on the wall. It's up to you. I'm not going to judge you. It's none of my business if you're driven by money or pursuit of power. Just remember, don't hurt anyone or yourself.

Here are the steps I suggest you follow:

1. Identify your most important needs

First of all, let's attend to those. You can use Maslow's pyramid of human needs (physiological - safety - love/belonging - esteem - self-actualisation, as help).

What is it that you need to have in order to feel happy? Are your basic needs such as food, shelter, and safety met? Or are you pursuing self-actualisation?

2. Identify your values

The drive to live a life aligned with your values is a powerful motivator. Explore your values -ask yourself the following questions:

- What is important to you? What do you value most in life?
- Think about what you really want out of life. What do you want your life to stand for? What do you want to do with your life?
- What sort of person do you want to be? What do you think your mission or purpose in this life is/are?

Also look at the following aspects of your life:

- What makes you happy and fulfilled? What do you truly enjoy doing? What would you do, even if no one paid you for it? What would you do if you had everything in life?

(Adapted from Chris Friesen's book *Achieve* - 7)

3. Explore what has driven your life so far

Look at what's motivated you in life so far. Rewards or avoiding punishment? Pursuing mastery (competence), autonomy, or a noble goal/bigger purpose?

Take your time when exploring these 3 areas. You can ask others for their views, but be careful not to let other people's opinions influence you too much.

4. Refine your findings

Look at your reflections and fine-tune them. Try to think about your drivers in terms of extrinsic and intrinsic motivators - assign them into the right categories.

5. Put it into categories

Further define which of the types of extrinsic and/or intrinsic motivators your drivers belong to. Is it rewards/punishment avoidance? Or autonomy, mastery, or purpose?

It's likely that you're driven by more than one type of motivation. Most people can identify some extrinsic and some intrinsic drivers. When it comes to intrinsic motivators, you may have a clear favourite, or feel that there is more than one thing that makes you tick. You can number them in the order of how powerful they are.

6. Test and tweak

As always, I encourage you to test your findings. You can set yourself a small goal and use the driver that you think is your most powerful motivation. Observe and note how it works. Have you completed your goal in no time, without even feeling like doing any kind of work? Did you feel energised, fulfilled, happy? Yes? You've got it right. No? Go through the exercise again, and test until you feel you've got it right.

Time to Take Action

If you're not sure what motivates you - invest time and effort into exploring it. The better you understand what makes you tick and use it appropriately to fuel your pursuits, the more likely you are to succeed at habit goals.

Go through the steps described above. Record your findings in your Workbook.

CHAPTER 23:
Dealing with Willpower Shortages and Outages

Since you've got here, you probably have a clear idea about my attitude towards motivation - assume you've got it, adjust your goals to fit with it, but don't bother with 'boosting' it.

Motivation is an unreliable strategy for establishing habits and creating a lasting change.

Okay, you may say, but what about those days when you really, really don't feel like following your routine?

Some habit mastery experts say that self-discipline and willpower are the way.

In his great book *Mini Habits*, (1) Stephen Guise writes about willpower being extremely reliable, as opposed to unreliable motivation. And if you have a force you can rely on, something that will make you turn up even when you don't feel like it, you can just schedule your new routine into your diary and - voila.

Sounds awesome. And if you have strong willpower - rejoice. Your journey to better habits is likely to be easier than for those of us who don't have such an iron self-control.

So what about those without a strong willpower? And what about those days when your willpower is down?

Let's look at those scenarios now.

Willpower is considered to be a limited resource (2). This hypothesis has been recently challenged (3), suggesting the amount of willpower available to an individual depends on their beliefs in relation to limitability of willpower (4). I don't know about you, but there are definitely moments in my life when my not-so-good willpower is in an even worse condition, whether I believe my willpower is limited or not.

So while scientists and psychologists seek further understanding how it all works, let's assume the worst - that willpower is limited - and let's look at the best ways of dealing with it.

Two main approaches to dealing with 'willpower outages' are:

- Preventing/minimising the likelihood of it happening
- Ensuring fast recovery

How to Prevent Willpower Shortages/Outages

Let's look at preventive strategies first.

1. Limit your choices

It looks like your willpower resource is used also when you're making choices and any decisions. Choosing one thing (or more) from a range of options means you are not choosing all the other options - and that requires some willpower to manage. That's why the more options you have, the harder the choice and the more detrimental the impact on your willpower reserves.

The solution is simple: limit the number of choices you make.

- **Limit the range of clothes you wear** - This is one of the most common approaches to limiting decision fatigue linked to too many choices. That's why many smart, successful people, such as Steve Jobs, Mark Zuckerberg, or Barack Obama limit the number of choices they have to make every day, by always wearing the same outfits (5).

Many people are following their suit and limiting the number of outfits in their wardrobes; too, some fashion designers even create fashion lines specifically designed to serve people like that (6).

- **Only buy stuff you absolutely need** - and be very clear on what you're looking for. Being clear on what you want to buy and only buying stuff you really need may reduce the time and effort required.

I hate shopping and prefer to do it online, because I can put my requirements into the browser and only focus on the stuff that meets them. I tend to stick to 1- 2 (3 when absolutely necessary) different retailers, and just stay within my limits.

- **Find ways of limiting your choices** - If you, like me, are price-sensitive - decide to buy only things that are on special or within a certain price range. Have rules for dealing with choices. For instance, if I'm offered a drink while out on a business, I ask for a glass of water.

2. Automate as many decisions as possible

Another way to limit the pressure on your decision-making and willpower resource is to automate as many decisions as you can.

Decide beforehand what you will eat/drink - If you decide on what to eat beforehand, you can lessen the burden on your willpower depletion/decision-fatigue. You can always eat the same thing for breakfast, or have 'breakfast by day of the week' (e.g. toast with jam on Mondays, scrambled egg on Tuesdays, etc., just like Sheldon Cooper from 'The Big Bang Theory' show).

Have a standard way of dealing with regular grocery shopping. For example, if you do your weekly shopping online - have your favourite buys saved and use them instead of browsing through the entire store of goods. Or only buy stuff that's the cheapest (price-sensitive option), or of a specific brand (brand loyalty option).

3. Create a system to bypass willpower issues

The best way to prevent willpower issues is to create a system that bypasses things that put pressure on your precious willpower resources.

The systems presented in this book are an example of what you can do. Please refer to the appropriate sections of this book for more information.

4. Flex your 'willpower muscle'

Willpower is like muscle. Fair enough, like a muscle it's fatigue-prone, but the upside is - it can be trained and strengthened (7). Interestingly, research shows that anything that strengthens your willpower in one area will strengthen your willpower in others. So, no matter what you choose as an exercise in building up your self-control, the positive effects of it will spill over other areas of your life.

Beumeister and Tieney suggest (7) 'willpower workouts' - any little exercises that will engage your willpower, such as controlling your body posture ('sitting with your back straight'), recording what you eat, switching to your non-dominant hand when opening doors, etc. Anything that challenges your habits and engages your willpower could be a good 'warm-up' and a step on your journey to further improving your willpower.

Interestingly, studies show that the best way to improve your willpower is through good old exercise. Kelly McGonigal, a health psychologist and the author of a very popular book on willpower, *The Willpower Instinct*, (9) argues that the willpower reserves are linked with heart rate (HR) variability - that is, the difference between your low and high heart rate - the higher the HR variability, the better the ability to control your impulses - 'willpower capacity.'

HR variability depends on many factors, including the environment you live in, stress levels, general health, and activities such as meditation, good sleep, and exercise can increase it.

I can definitely vouch for exercise - ever since I started exercise regularly, I've noticed that my ability to resist temptation improved, including temptation not to go out for a run and sweets. And yes, my HR variability also increased.

If you want to strengthen your willpower, keep reading - there are some juicy tips on building your willpower in the next Chapter.

5. Ensure your body is prepared for willpower use

The level of willpower in your tank seems to be linked with the level of glucose (sugar) in your blood (10), or as the newer evidence suggests - the sweet sensation in your mouth (11). And again, while scientists and psychologist are clarifying what really matters here (12), you may consider minimising the possibilities of willpower 'shortages and outages' by ensuring an appropriate nutrition for your brain (13).

Now you know how to minimise the likelihood of your willpower running low when you need it. However, even with the best care taken, you may still come across situations when your ability to control yourself is down or low. Let's now look at dealing with these.

How to Recover from Willpower Outages

First of all - good news: willpower is renewable. And the first step to recovering from a 'willpower outage' is to recognise when it happens.

If you feel like you 'can't be bothered' to push yourself harder, or make any more decisions, if you feel an urge to defer any decision-making or choice-making, this is a likely sign of a willpower depletion.

This is what you can do to help yourself recover from it:

1. Avoid decision-making

Avoid or delay decision-making, if possible, until your willpower supply has replenished itself. Yes, it's as simple as that - put it off until your full faculties are back on. Otherwise you may regret decisions made during the period of low willpower supply.

2. Take time to recover

Willpower takes time to replenish itself. Don't panic - it's normal and it will happen. Accept this is the reality and... chill out.

Willpower is an ability to control your impulses, and as such belongs to the area of your brain called the prefrontal cortex. Chilling out, resting, sleeping, or just simply doing whatever you enjoy without any need for restricting your impulses or choices may help.

Sleep deprivation is particularly hard on our ability to control impulses - McGonigal (8) even calls it 'mild prefrontal dysfunction' - as it is associated with the loss of control and impairs higher functions of our brain (the ones located in the prefrontal cortex).

McGonigal also suggests '5-minute green willpower fill-up' - a short walk in a park, or a little bit of gardening.

The bottom line - any type of relaxation can help you restore your willpower supply.

3. In emergencies – oral glucose boost

This one really is for emergencies only. Since the level of willpower in your tank seems to have a connection to the level of sugar in your blood or that sweet taste in your mouth, in a time of emergency you may consider a quick sweet snack or just rinsing your mouth with a sweet drink (a sweetened tea/coffee, soft drink, or just a glass of sugary water).

Personally, although the scientific evidence is not as robust as it was originally claimed, I am inclined to believe that boosting my glucose levels helps me restore my willpower reserves. Given the mixed scientific evidence as well as health downsides related to this approach, I recommend you exercise your own judgement before using it.

Just be careful and use this strategy with caution. Unfortunately, I've used this approach far too much, relying on snacking much more often than my dentist and my clothes would like. I believe that my current problems with weight and teeth are at least partially related to me abusing this strategy. I realise this is the case and have been working on making my willpower reserves more sustainable. I have been successfully using walks, naps, and guilt-free sessions of my favourite silly mobile game instead.

As usual, I urge you to exercise your own judgement when

choosing your strategies for dealing with willpower problems. Since prevention is always better than cure, look at your current decision-making commitments and try to limit what you can. As for willpower-restoring strategies - start with the proven ones and check if they work for you.

Next, Martin Meadows, a bestselling author of multiple books on personal growth and particularly on self-discipline will show you how you can build lasting willpower.

HACK YOUR HABITS

CHAPTER 24:
Guest Expert Chapter – Martin Meadows – 5 Unusual but Effective Strategies to Build Lasting Willpower

Martin Meadows is a bestselling author and a personal growth aficionado. He is one of my favourite writers on all matters willpower and self-discipline. His strategies are effective and his approach to presenting them - very practical and down-to-earth. I have personally used a number of them. Here, Martin shares with you 5 less-known, but effective approaches to building lasting willpower. No 1 and 4 are my current favourites and I can already see positive effects of them.

For many people, lasting willpower is elusive. Dealing with cravings when you're on a diet or addressing the temptation to slack off when you should be working can be intense. We all know that choosing the comfort of the sofa instead of putting on workout gear can be overpowering.

How can you build willpower to deal with these common problems? Here are five unusual, but effective strategies to help you:

1. Wait On It

Waiting on the temptation for fifteen minutes is often enough to diminish the craving to a manageable level. The key to make it work is focusing on something else rather than trying <u>not</u> to think about a temptation.

Try <u>not</u> to think about a pink elephant now. You just visualized a pink elephant, didn't you? Suppressing thoughts doesn't work. Redirect your focus instead.

If you feel like eating chocolate cake, distract yourself by putting on your running shoes and going for a run. If you're about to put an unhealthy item in your shopping cart, go to an aisle with fresh produce instead and distract yourself by choosing vegetables for dinner.

Alternately, sometimes telling yourself that you <u>will</u> give in after you wait fifteen minutes is enough to regain composure, because the craving ceases to be a forbidden fruit.

2. Think of the Consequences

Humans find it difficult to understand how it feels to be in an opposite state than the one in which they are at the moment.

If you're not hungry, you can't imagine yourself not being able to turn down a slice of pizza. If you have a lot of energy, it's hard to understand why sometimes you can't get off the couch and go exercise. If you feel motivated to work, you wonder how it's possible you often procrastinate so much.

It's difficult to think of the negative consequences when you're craving something. Make mental notes of the consequences after giving in to a temptation (like 'I feel exhausted and lazy when I spend four hours in front of the TV instead of doing my workout and meeting with a friend'), then remind yourself of those consequences when you feel like giving in again.

If you have a tendency to skip workouts, note the next time how disappointed you feel in yourself. Then remind yourself of this feeling when you're tempted to give yourself a break again. It might be enough to draw out enough willpower to train.

3. Do It Now

When you procrastinate, you choose a little reward – temporary comfort – at the expense of long-term peace of mind. In the end, you suffer more because sooner or later, you'll be forced to take action, and this time, it will be even harder to start.

Deal with the temptation to procrastinate by modifying your default response to it.

Imagine you've finished eating dinner. You look at the dishes that need washing and say to yourself, 'I want to finish watching my TV series. I'll wash them later.'

Stop.

Pause the series and do it now. By overcoming the temptation to get a small reward now (watching your series), you forgo a bigger reward – watching your series without the unpleasant thought of the dishes you still need to wash.

Do you need to make an unpleasant call? Do it now and be done with it. A few minutes from now, you can relax instead of worrying that you still have to make the call.

Don't feel like working out? Change into your workout clothes and go to the gym right away. It will be harder to go exercise in ten minutes, so why make yourself suffer more?

Tempted to call it a day before finishing your most important task? Get it done now and have peace of mind. The satisfying feeling will be more than worth it – and you'll also avoid the horrible feeling of wasting your day.

The more times you repeat the simple behaviour of doing unpleasant things immediately, the more automated your response gets. Soon, you'll train yourself to forgo little, immediate rewards and automatically choose the more fulfilling, delayed gratification.

4. Practice Suffering

If you're reading this book, your life is most likely incomparably easier than the lives of millions of people who lack access to fresh water, abundant food, safety, and peace.

That's not to say your life doesn't come with challenges – it does. However, generally speaking, your life is devoid of many discomforts others experience on a daily basis.

Since you aren't used to true hardships, small roadblocks

might appear insurmountable to you when in reality, they aren't that challenging.

And no, I'm not singling you out. My life is also comfortable. That's why I practice suffering to get myself accustomed to hardships. Then, whenever I face problems, I can draw from my experiences of self-imposed discomfort.

Some of the prime exercises you can do to toughen yourself up include:

Please bear in mind that I'm not a doctor. You should always consult a trained professional if you would like to expose your body to something that might be uncomfortable, like some of the strategies listed below – especially if you suffer from any health disorders.

- Taking ice-cold showers. Exposing yourself to cold leads to a rapid and intense spike in adrenaline, provoking a reaction that you <u>must</u> escape it. If you can bear it, though, you'll learn how to cope with your physical weaknesses, which will help you whenever you deal with other challenging events.
- Engaging in intermittent fasting. When you abstain from food for a longer period of time – say, 16 to 24 hours – you'll definitely feel hunger and subsequent discomfort. As you let the feeling go and continue your fast, you'll teach yourself you have control over your urges. When repeated numerous times, you'll become a master at staying disciplined despite discomfort.
- Doing strenuous physical exercise. When you push your

physical limits and go beyond them, you work your self-control like a muscle. Any demanding, exhausting sport is a great way to practice suffering. I suggest weightlifting, martial arts, sprints, swimming, or high-intensity interval training.

- Purposefully doing things that make you uncomfortable. If you're terrified of public speaking, join a Toastmasters group and learn how to present in front of a lot of people. If you're afraid of heights, try skydiving, bungee jumping, or climbing. From time to time, make yourself uncomfortable by eating a plain diet for a day or two, sleeping on the floor, leaving your phone at home, living without your car for a few days, or standing while you work.

All these exercises will teach you how to be comfortable with discomfort. This ability will be of immense help whenever you face the real struggles and hardships life throws at you.

5. Switch Excuses for Honesty

It's easier to give in to a temptation after coming up with an excuse – even the silliest one.

'Oh, it's raining. I can't go running.'

'My friend wants to eat pizza. I'll cheat this time because she'll get mad if I choose a healthy salad instead.'

'It's already past 8 pm I won't work on my business today because it's too late, and my favourite TV series is airing soon.'

Be real with yourself and switch your excuses for honesty.

You're not going to watch TV instead of running because it's raining. Don't use rain as your scapegoat. The only true reason why you won't run is because you lack willpower to do it.

Investigate whether you're being really honest with yourself or if these supposedly good reasons are just weak excuses to rationalize your lack of willpower. Being mindful of this fact might help you overcome your lack of self-control and do the unpleasant things despite your weak willpower.

(This is an excerpt from Martin's great audio course: Supercharge Your Self-Discipline, (1)

HACK YOUR HABITS

Chapter 25:
What to Do When Life Gets in the Way

But what if things get off track?

We've talked about the importance of keeping an eye on your system's performance, from the strategies you use to target specific focus problems, to your habit loop and its Cue and Reward, etc. Hopefully this will be enough to keep you going, at least for some time.

In this chapter, I wanted to give you a few tips on what to do when things start getting off track after a while, or your life circumstances change.

So you have your habit designed and it's working like a dream. That's great. And it keeps going like a dream for a while, until one day you realise you've missed your Routine a couple of times too many. You make some adjustments, try harder, but it's just not the same.

Your habit system is not working as well as it used to.

What's happened?

Most likely - the usual: life.

Life goes on and our needs change. Even with the best-designed system, there may be times when something major happens in your life and/or your environment changes. It may be things such as moving house, or having visitors staying with you for longer than a few days, or you go away on holiday. If your system is well set up and none of the key elements is affected, then you should be able to return to your Routine as soon as your life returns to normal.

However, sometimes there will be situations when your Routine is affected in a more permanent way.

One of my previous students had a sick relative moving in with her. Someone else bought a bigger house and needed more furniture. These are quite common scenarios, but they affect your environment. And with a major life event, such as moving in with a new life partner, or having a baby, your Routine is completely disrupted.

As a result, your context changes, your needs change, and what's worked for you so far is no longer as effective as it used to be.

Things like that will happen, because that's part of life. But be mindful that your habit system will also be affected. So it is crucial that you **recognise when it happens and adjust your system to cater to your changed needs or changed life circumstances.**

The key thing is to realise when **a temporary change has become more permanent**, and make appropriate adjustments in your system.

The best way to go about it is to follow the framework again:

1. What's Your Habit Problem?

Often, when major life changes are involved, our priorities and perspectives shift. It's not unusual to realise that something that used to be a problem no longer is, or a minor inconvenience has just grown to an immense, insurmountable mountain of an issue.

Examples?

If you just moved jobs and your new office is no longer a cubicle in an open-plan space, but a proper one, your productivity routine with headphones and white noise that kept you focused on the job at hand may no longer necessary, but you may have a different set of productivity challenges.

Or if your new boyfriend just moved in with you, your morning exercise habits have been put on hold.

Or, if you happened to just have a baby, getting a decent night's sleep is no longer a matter of setting a reminder up to go to bed earlier, but it's become a massive problem of its own.

If you experienced any changes in your life, and daily routine in particular, ask yourself: what is the problem you want to address. As always, be open and honest with yourself when thinking about it, because the better you diagnose the problem, the more likely you are to solve it.

2. What do You Want to Achieve? What's Your Desired Outcome?

This is the key question, even more important than the 'What's your problem' question discussed above. And honesty in answering it is even more important than at any other point in the system.

Yes, your life may have changed, and suddenly what used to work for you is no longer working. But don't just assume this is a problem, because it may be not be.

If your morning exercise routine has gone out of the window because you prefer, eh, sleeping in in the morning now that your boyfriend is living with you - that's a change in preferences. And yes, you may still want to continue with daily exercise, but maybe not necessarily in the morning.

And if your usual focus routine is not working, because you have a different office setup, you may need to review what you want to achieve, what is that desired outcome you're seeking?

With your own office, do you still need white noise to help you focus on your work? Or have your issues changed and now, without people looking over your shoulder all the time, you don't feel the pressure to work and procrastinate much more?

Look at your situation and what you believe to be the problem - what do you want to achieve by addressing it?

3. Is This Realistic/Achievable?

Once you've identified your new, revised Desired Outcome, consider carefully if your goal is achievable and realistic in the given context. Be mindful when considering your context, as it has changed.

Consider all aspects of your current context: physical (e.g. new office setup, much less noise), internal (your emotional and mental states, e.g., the effects of having fewer boundaries and hence being more prone to mind wandering) and social (no distractions caused by office mates, but also no pressure of your office mates looking over your shoulder).

Is your new goal realistic and achievable in this new context?

Sometimes, it's a matter of some minor tweaks; for example, you may want to shift your exercise routine from morning to evening to accommodate your plan to spend mornings with your boyfriend. But sometimes you will need to abandon or substantially review some of your goals.

If your life circumstances changed substantially, particularly when it comes to your physical, internal, or social environment, **you would likely need to review your goal**.

For example, if your productivity/focus routine relied on the fact that at any point any of your office mates could look over your shoulder, moving into your own space suddenly rendered this strategy invalid. No more eyes watching you. You probably need to either revise your old system to include an element of social/peer pressure or start from scratch.

Go through the steps described in Chapter 6 as many times as you need until you reach a realistic and achievable goal you're confident about.

4. Adjust Your System

Depending on the results of your realistic and achievable goal exercise, and any potential changes in your context, you may need to adjust your system, either in terms of your Habit Loop, your Habit Plan, or fail-/future-proofing of your solution.

Below are a few typical scenarios when you need to adjust the system and how to go about it.

Cue and Reward changes in Habit Loop

With your environment, particularly internal and social, changed, you may need to change your Cue and/or Reward.

Any changes in your physical environment may result in a need to adjust your Cue and how it works. Again, try to put the Cue in your environment, or use a tool. Check Chapter 13 for suggestions.

If you find that your Rewards are no longer effective, you may need to review them again. Go through Chapter 15 again and choose a new Reward you think is likely to drive you in your new context. Remember about the importance of being honest with yourself, and the power of putting the right fuel into your tank. Be careful with extrinsic rewards.

Fail- and future-proofing your system

Your proofing of the adjusted system may also need a review. Depending on your new challenges, on your limitations and constraints, you may need to adapt your routine, using different strategies and tricks to ensure your system always works for you. Just go over Part 5 and consider carefully what may work for you.

5. Test and Tweak Your System

As always, test it and don't shy away from tweaking or dumping strategies that are ineffective, or bring too little return on investment, no matter how effective they were for anyone else, or in the past. Be mindful with your context being different than before, your expected returns on investment may also be different.

Be kind to yourself. Any major life change, whether happy or not, always adds to your stress levels. Don't expect your new system to work as well as the previous one straightaway. It may take more time to kick in, or you may need to settle for lower ROI than before. Give yourself more time to experiment with your new system, and accept that it's likely to be a slow process.

It may be you need to settle for something less than optimal, but you can at least devise a system you can live with. Keep a careful eye on your system, and if you feel more comfortable in your new situation, try tweaking it. Change one element at a time so you can identify what's worked and what hasn't and further improve your system until you're happy with it.

HACK YOUR **HABITS**

Chapter 26:
Help, My Support System Isn't Very Supportive

Lack of social support is a common factor that prevents people from creating healthy habits or breaking bad ones. It is particularly prominent when it comes to barriers to physical activity and healthy eating choices - showing lack of social support as the most common perceived barrier (1, 2).

Yes, change is hard, also for those around you.

System's Resistance to Change

If you're part of a system (and unless you live on a desert island, you are), any change you attempt to make may result in the system's resistance. If you wonder why - just imagine yourself being a cog in the machine your family or workplace is (I know, it's painful, but bear with me for a minute), and other people around you are parts of the machine too. The machine is working, even if it's imperfect. If one of the cogs (i.e. you) starts turning slower, faster, in the opposite direction, or in some other way starts behaving differently, the balance in the whole machine/system is upset.

That's why, in most cases, at least initially, your nearest and dearest, even though they intellectually support your change for the better, may have difficulty adjusting to it on the emotional level.

Dealing with Resistance and Hostility

Support is very important to success in personal change, such as habit creation, but what's worse than lack of support is resistance and hostility.

S.J. Scott, a habit expert and the author of *Bad Habits No More* (3) advises that, 'Sadly, there will be people who will subconsciously (or consciously) try to sabotage your effort at self-improvement.' These could be random strangers, or family and friends, and 'their words can poison, because they'll flood your mind with self-doubt and limiting beliefs.' The key to successfully dealing with all those 'naysayers,' according to Scott, is to have a plan for handling them - knowing what to say and what to do. He suggests finding a way to ignore or immediately brush off those comments.

Scott also suggests using If-Then planning (check 'Chapter 18 for suggestions on how to use it) for those instances, and gives a few examples of ignoring or immediately 'rebuffing' the comments (e.g. politely changing the subject, 'muting' or 'unfriending' an unsupportive friend on social media). However, he also advises care when it comes to choosing who you surround yourself with when working on building better habits.

Leo Babuta of ZenHabits has his own method of dealing with others who don't share his lifestyle choices (simplifying his life).

His approach (4) is that of patiently and tactfully trying to get people on your side, by gently educating about the positive impact of your new behaviour, its importance to you, modelling the new behaviour, and inviting them to join you on your journey, if possible. However, if it's not possible, Babauta advises to accept that you can't control or change others. He suggests setting boundaries to allow you to co-exist peacefully in the same space, e.g, splitting the office or finding a compromise.

Ignore Naysayers and Seek Alternative Support

If your nearest and dearest don't support your goals, you may need to find support elsewhere.

Martin Meadows, a bestselling author and an expert on self-discipline, writes that the most useful approach to dealing with unsupportive people in your life is to focus on yourself and ignore what others are saying. He also advises surrounding yourself with people who share your attitude (5), by e.g. joining a group of people who share your enthusiasm for your exercise type/sport activity, whether it's in a form of a gym/club, or an Internet forum/group.

Martin's book, *How to Build Self-Discipline to Exercise*, is focused on exercise; however, I believe his advice on seeking support can be extrapolated to any other good habit area. The Internet is great for facilitating connections among people who would have not met otherwise - people from far-flung places, different cultures and ages, but sharing the same passion and enthusiasm or commitment to the change.

Start by checking your existing social network for people who may be working towards similar habit goals or considering a change. Ask people you trust for recommendations. With any habit that has an effect on your health, consider consulting your doctor, or another trusted health professional, or a trusted source. You can also post a question on your social networks, reach out to those who you know may be doing it or may consider doing it.

Check your favourite social media outlet by running a search: your habit building/breaking + support group/community, e.g. healthy eating (habit) support group/forum.

You can try searching for specific support groups/clubs in your area, or online. Be careful when choosing the groups/forums: check their credentials, read some posts before you join, and be careful when posting. Beware of false experts, people posing as experts, and cults. As someone with a scientific background, I also suggest you stick to scientific and proven approaches. Use your judgement, common sense, and stay safe when posting.

In this chapter we discussed what you can do if your nearest and dearest don't support you in your efforts to build better habits. In the next chapter we'll look at another common issue - the 'what-the-hell' effect.

CHAPTER 27:
'What the Hell?' Effect, and Getting Back on Track

We've all been there. You get to a point where you slip up and eat that chocolate bar you swore not to eat, spend more than the allocated time checking your emails, or hit the snooze button instead of getting up early to meditate. The slip-up is minor, and as such, not a threat to your goal (1), but this is the riskiest point on your road to a better you.

If you just finish that bar and go back to your regular healthy eating for the rest of the day, or keep browsing the Net or lie-in for another 10 minutes and then go back to your work/get up - it's not a problem. We all make mistakes, we all have bad days and slip-ups. And if you just 'chalk it up' as such and go back to pursuing your habit goals, that's fine.

The real issue is when your craving brain tells you: 'Ah, screw it. You've already 'committed the crime,' you may as well enjoy it.' And you go 'the whole hog' - have another chocolate bar and then finish off the pizza from the night before; or procrastinate for the next hour, or pull the blanket over your head and doze off. This is the **'what-the-hell' effect**.

'What-the-hell effect' (WTH effect) is actually quite common, particularly among dieters (2, 3) - once you believe (whether correctly or not) you've overeaten, you're much more likely to go on overeating.

But people who try to budget are prone to it, too (4), as well as anyone else working towards goals that require self-discipline and willpower. Initial self-control failure is likely to trigger more of the undesired behaviour.

Be aware of WTH effect. The name may be funny, but it's real. I'm guilty of falling for WTH effect, too, particularly when it comes to limiting my sweets/carbs. It's hard to stop eating those yummy marshmallows, or leave the rest of the cake for tomorrow/someone else.

How to Deal with WTH

How you deal with it may depend on the specific goal you're pursuing, as well as your context. As usual, **being aware and mindful of it is the first step**.

Forgiving yourself the lapse and stopping before it becomes a major relapse is a good strategy, too (5).

Missing a day in your routine does not pose a major threat to your habit (1). But **beware of skipping more than one day**. Once is a happenstance, twice is a coincidence, but it may start becoming a pattern, but three - you've got a problem.

If you notice those slip-ups becoming too frequent, consider reviewing your system. If your system is not delivering on the promise more often than acceptable, there is something wrong with it. First, diagnose what the underlying problem may be and then try to address it.

The most common reasons are lack of adequate fail-proofing, choice of strategies that don't work for you, or even more fundamental - pursuing the wrong goal, or the right goal but at the wrong time or in an unsupportive environment.

If you frequently find yourself battling with WTH effect - review your system and adjust its elements if necessary.

In the early days of establishing my morning study routine, I would quite often try to 'study on the sofa' and fall asleep, only to wake up in the middle of the night and cause the whole system to collapse. At that time, I had a big poster with 'I'll start again tomorrow' up on the wall - a leftover from my constant battles with a sugar-fuelled diet. The aim of it was to keep trying every day. But I realised the promise of 'tomorrow' (there is always tomorrow and - thank goodness, it's not today) was creating more problems that it helped. I didn't know about the WTH effect then, but I had a sense it was a way of procrastinating. So I took the poster down and replaced it with a 'Start again from now' note.

I continue using this approach to this day. Have I eaten too many marshmallows? Oops. I'd better stop eating them, and start again from now.

SJ Scott, (6) also suggests using specific short-term goals with small wins to overcome those small slip-ups, keeping a log of slip-ups. Use the following strategies to minimise the likelihood of WTH effect ruining your hard work.

Pull Yourself Back on Track

Slip-ups will happen - that's just the way life is. Don't spend too much time crying over them, but recognise they will happen and prepare yourself. People with realistic attitudes to self-improvement are more likely to achieve their goals (7). Pull yourself back on track as soon as you can. The earlier you do it, the easier it will be. Don't worry about the performance - just pull all your energy to get back into the swing of things, writes James Clear (8).

Now we've covered a common problem of abandoning your goals in face of a minor slip-up, the so-called 'what-the-hell-effect,' we'll look at some strategies to build up your willpower.

Part 7:

Bonus Tips and Tricks for Building Better Habits into Your Life

- Introduction to this section

- Chapter 28:   Focus on a Keystone Habit to Transform Your Life

- Chapter 29:   Guest Expert Chapter - Hal Elrod - How to Build a Miracle Morning Routine in 6 Minutes

- Chapter 30:   Guest Expert Chapter - Steve S.J. Scott - How to Stack Small Habits for A Powerful Impact

Introduction to this section

This section of the book is dedicated to strategies that will help you build your new habits into your life. Whether you're wondering which habits to focus on first, feel you don't have time for a morning routine, or would like to implement several little routines - you will find well-tested advice, tips, and tricks here.

CHAPTER 28:
Focus on a Keystone Habit to Transform Your Life

Are you overwhelmed with the feeling you've got too many habits to fix? You'd love to start building healthy routines and don't know where to start?

I know the feeling. I'll show you how you can transform your life by picking the right habit to focus on first.

Twenty years ago I did something that transformed my life. Literally overnight, I went from constantly tired, overworked, stressed and pass-grade student to a happy, energetic, bright-eyed and bushy-tailed A-grader.

I shifted from studying on the sofa/bed in the evening to getting up early and sitting at the desk.

The change from trying to read textbooks while lying in bed/on the sofa to doing it at the desk dramatically reduced my propensity to fall asleep while studying. It looks pretty simple and obvious , but the ripple-effect that this simple change created was massive and went well beyond that simple rule.

Suddenly, my study sessions were more effective (I was

spending more time doing the actual work rather than dozing on and off), which then freed up more time for sleep. And since my study sessions were shifted to the morning, I could go to bed earlier and actually get some decent sleep. With better sleep, I felt more energetic and more productive in the morning. Moreover, I realised I quite enjoyed mornings and discovered I was more of a morning person than an owl. Aligning my natural energy flow with my work/study schedule further increased the effectiveness of my sessions.

This then led to even more powerful results and me jumping out of bed every morning, happy and looking forward to the day.

Who would have thought that such a simple change can create such powerful and lasting effects?

This is how my morning routine was born. Now, twenty years later, I still get up in the morning, regardless of how little sleep I had the night before, and still look forward to the day. It's my favourite time of day, to the point that I prefer to sacrifice the amount of sleep I get so I can get up early and enjoy it.

The other night after a very busy evening, I happened to forget to put my alarm on and ended up sleeping in. Even though I didn't have to get up early and enjoyed the extra 90 minutes of sleep, I was devastated - my favourite part of the day was gone.

My morning routine is an example of what Charles Duhigg (1) calls **the keystone habit.**

Keystone Habits

Keystone habits are behaviours, which can serve as a platform for any other habits to grow and develop from; habits that can have the most powerful impact on our lives and on our performance, our results.

They will be different for each of us, not only because we are different, but because we have different priorities in life. Our keystone habits reflect our personality, core values, and priorities.

Keystone habits, as Duhigg (1) writes, are habits that influence 'how we people work, eat, play, live, spend and communicate. Keystone habits start a process that, over time, transforms everything'. These are habits that can shift other patterns and create a ripple effect with the power to transform our lives.

But identifying keystone habits can be tricky.

According to Duhigg, successful keystone-habit formation relies on identifying relevant priorities and using them as powerful levers.

Research says keystone habits have the following qualities:

- They create opportunities for small wins that can cumulate to create powerful momentum
- They serve as a platform for other habits to develop and grow
- They give us a sense of excellence, energy, and confidence to go further in self-improvement

In essence: these are those habits that change your life, not only through the benefits they bring, but enabling you to implement other good habits.

Keystone Habit Examples

For James Clear, habit and behaviour change writer, the keystone habit was his exercise routine (2).

For me, a keystone habit was to start getting up in the morning to study. It started as a necessity - I wanted my study sessions to be more productive. But as I began getting up in the morning, I started going to bed earlier, so the quantity and quality of my sleep improved. That helped me learn faster and more effectively - just with the power of sleep. So my main aim for creating a study routine was achieved, but this was not the end of benefits.

On top of that I discovered pleasures of the morning cup of coffee, the quiet house, watching the beautiful morning sky. I started looking forward to those moments, as my favourite time of day. Which, in turn, got me ready to face the day with a positive attitude - giving me strength and energy to deal with whatever life threw at me. I became a happier person. With my studying now happening in the morning, I had time and energy in the afternoons and evenings to do other things, such as spending time with friends and enjoying my hobbies. I even found time for work, which brought in extra money that I needed so badly.

This is how a small change created a massive shift in my life.

Common examples of keystone habits are:

- Regular exercise
- Good sleep routine
- Healthier eating habits
- Journaling
- Meditation/mindfulness practice

Find Your Keystone Habit

I challenge to find your own keystone habit and start from there. Examine your current situation and look for those aspects of your life you feel are holding you back from becoming a better version of yourself. Look for things in your control, though - elements of your daily routines with a power to create a ripple-effect. Usually, these are all those 'if I could only's, or 'why don't you just?'s that you hear from your nearest and dearest.

Be open in your explorations, because you may well come across a well-ingrained problem, and obstacles that are often more in your mind than in reality.

Remember, you're looking for an area of improvement in your life where you can start reaping rewards quickly ('small wins'), but that has a potential to ignite that chain reaction for more positive changes.

Let me use a sleep routine as an example: with a better sleep routine, the quality and quantity of your sleep can quickly improve. That will make you feel rested, more energetic and happier in the morning. Your productivity will improve, but also your mood. Being less cranky will make it easier to deal with other people, so your relationships with your family, friends or colleagues will improve. As you can see, we already have a lot of little wins. But with that on board, there is more room for further steps. As a result, you will return home less tired and may have time and energy to exercise. And if you start exercising, you will feel better physically and mentally, with more energy and enthusiasm to implement other changes. All that started with the single step - improving your sleep routine.

Once you've identified an area that has the potential to become a keystone habit, go through the steps described earlier in the book - all the rules still apply.

CHAPTER 29:
Guest Expert Chapter – Hal Elrod – How to Build a Miracle Morning Routine in 6 Minutes

After he came back from death and then turned around from a financial and emotional crash, Hal Elrod wrote an inspirational story not only of his return and following success, but more importantly, of a powerful yet simple framework for a morning routine that anyone can use.

Hal's #1 bestselling book, The Miracle Morning: The Not-So-Obvious Secret to Transform Your Life (Before 8AM), *has helped millions change their lives for the better.*

Below, Hal shares the secrets of his 6-step Miracle Morning routine to help you transform your life in just 6 minutes.

> 'On the one hand, we all want to be happy. On the other hand, we all know the things that make us happy. But we don't do those things. Why? Simple. We are too busy. Too busy doing what? Too busy trying to be happy.'
>
> Matthew Kelly, Bestselling Author

Oh, you're busy? Weird, I thought it was just me.

No matter where you are in life at this moment, there is at least one thing that you and I have in common: we want to improve our lives and ourselves. I'm not saying there's anything wrong with us, but as human beings we're born with a desire to continuously grow and improve. I believe it's within all of us. Yet most people wake up each day and life pretty much stays the same.

If success and fulfilment were measured on a scale of 1 to 10, it's safe to say that everyone would want to live every aspect of their lives at a Level 10.

Here's the catch: To create the Level 10 life that you ultimately want, you must first dedicate time each day to becoming a Level 10 person who is capable of creating and sustaining that level of success.

But who has time for that, right? Luckily, there is a method to do it in as little as six minutes a day.

Enter the life SAVERS, a sequence that combines the six most effective personal development practices known to man: Silence, Affirmations, Visualisation, Exercise, Reading and Scribing. [1]

Of course, you can spend as much time as you want or can afford to on each of these 6 steps, but it only takes one minute for each - or six minutes' total - to see extraordinary results. So for days when you're extra busy, or for those of you overwhelmed with your life situation at the moment, here is an example of a 6-minute Miracle Morning:

Minute One... (Silence)

Imagine waking up in the morning, and instead of rushing carelessly into your hectic day—feeling stressed and overwhelmed—you instead spend the first minute sitting in purposeful Silence. You sit, very calm, very peaceful, and you breathe deeply, slowly. Maybe you say a prayer of gratitude to appreciate the moment, or pray for guidance on your journey. Maybe, you decide to try your first minute of meditation. As you sit in silence, you're totally present in the now, in the moment. You calm your mind, relax your body, and allow all of your stress to melt away. You develop a deeper sense of peace, purpose, and direction...

Minute Two... (Affirmations)

You pull out your daily Affirmations—the ones that remind you of your unlimited potential and your most important priorities—and you read them out loud from top to bottom. As you focus on what's most important to you, your level of internal motivation increases. Reading over the reminders of how capable you really are gives you a feeling of confidence. Looking over what you're committed to, what your purpose is, and what your goals are re-energizes you to take the actions necessary to live the life you truly want, deserve, and now know is possible for you...

Minute Three... (Visualization)

You close your eyes, or you look at your vision board, and you visualize. Your Visualization could include your goals, what it will look and feel like when you reach them. You visualize the day going perfectly, see yourself enjoying your work, smiling and laughing with your family, or your significant other, and easily accomplishing all that you intend to accomplish for that day. You see what it will look like, you feel what it will feel like, and you experience the joy of what you will create...

Minute Four... (Scribing)

Imagine, pull out your journal, and in your journal, you take a minute to write down what you're grateful for, what you're proud of, and the results you're committed to creating for that day. Doing so, you put yourself in an empowered, inspired, and confident state of mind.

Minute Five... (Reading)

Then, you grab your self-help book and invest one miraculous minute reading a page or two. You learn a new idea, something that you can implement into your day. You discover something new that you can use to feel better—to be better.

Minute Six... (Exercise)

Finally, you stand up and you spend the last minute, doing jumping jacks for 60 seconds and getting your heart rate up, getting energized, waking yourself up, and increasing your ability to be alert and to focus.

See, your morning routine doesn't have to be long or

arduous. I bet even the busiest person in the world can find 6 minutes every day.

Investing this tiny chunk of time into your personal development is not only reasonable, but also indispensable if you truly want to achieve that Level 10 life. You may be pleasantly surprised when you see just how POWERFUL (and life-changing) these six minutes can be.

Go on. Implement the SAVERS and change your life, one morning at a time.

-Hal Elrod

Bestselling Author of The Miracle Morning (1, 2, 3)

HACK YOUR HABITS

CHAPTER 30:
Guest Expert Chapter – Steve S.J. Scott - How to Stack Small Habits for A Powerful Impact

Steve S.J. Scott is a best-selling author and a habit expert. His goal is to help people learn how to build a better life - one habit at a time. His approach to habit-building is practical and very down-to-earth and his habit-stacking strategy is one of my personal favourites. If you feel overwhelmed by a number of little routines you want to implement into your life - fear not. Steve has a great idea how to do it. Read on to see how.

Everyone has their own personal habits. Some can be good, such as writing, exercising, or eating that piece of fruit. Others can be extremely damaging, such as smoking, losing your temper, or cheating on your spouse. What's interesting is it's easy to notice the big habits and forget all about those small things that we do on a daily basis.

As an example, you probably brush your teeth. This habit doesn't take that long and isn't that hard to do. In fact, even the busiest, most overwhelmed people in the world find five minutes of time to properly brush their teeth. Unfortunately, it's hard to say the same thing about other equally miniscule habits that could have a positive impact on our lives.

Think about this: How much would your life improve if you were able to add the following: de-cluttering your house, buying your wife flowers while grocery shopping, complimenting a stranger, tracking your daily expenses, or eating that darn piece of fruit?

We all have been inundated with reminders about how these activities are important, but seriously, how often do you *actually* do them?

Probably not very often.

Don't Have Time?

The most common excuse for not taking action is *time*. Many people feel like there are simply not enough hours in the day to get things done. However, if you go back to the teeth brushing example, then you know that 'limited time' is simply an excuse we give for activities we feel aren't immediately important. You have enough time to brush those pearly whites, so why aren't you able to add other quality habits?

Can't Remember?

I think the answer stems from something called *cognitive load*. We have a finite limit on our short-term memories. You can only retain a small amount of information and have to rely on long-term memory, habits, and established processes to do basically everything in life.

Think back to that small list of life changes. You know that de-cluttering your home and randomly complimenting a stranger could be beneficial. But these activities are easy to forget because they're not part of an established, daily framework.

The Purpose of Habit Stacking

Habit stacking helps you develop simple, easy to implement routines that link various, short habits, and are managed by checklists.

Linking habits together is a way of getting more done in less time, resulting in a positive change in your life. As you perform the stacked actions every day, they become part of your daily routine.

With this strategy you don't have to worry about cognitive load because all you have to remember is to **follow the checklist**. So even if you're completely stressed out, you'll still find the time and energy to complete these quick habits on a consistent basis.

Big Doors Swing on Little Hinges

You'll find that implementing small changes can have a significant impact on your life. By completing dozens of small habits on a daily basis, you'll be able to make giant leaps forward in your business, strengthen your personal relationships, stay on top of your finances, get organized and improve your health.

Below are key elements of habit stacking strategy to help you create those time- and energy-saving little changes that can transform your life in 30 minutes or less.

8 Elements of a Habit Stacking Routine

Element #1: Each habit takes less than five minutes to complete

Each habit within your habit-stacking routine takes less than five minutes to complete. This means each task is simple and doesn't require a major time commitment, making it easy to finish and move on to the next habit.

A great example of a quick one-minute habit is collecting all your loose change and adding it to a change jar, or sending a text message to a friend that you haven't connected with in a while

Element #2: It's a complete habit

A complete habit is an action that cannot be built upon. For example, exercising is a habit that can be built upon. Exercises change, increase or decrease, and develop over time. This is not the point of a habit within habit stacking. Each habit is a full action completed in a short amount of time— like making your bed. It is basically the same action every day and doesn't vary much in the time it takes to complete.

Element #3: It improves your life

Habit stacking is done with the purpose of improving your life. The positive changes that come along with habit stacking are reflected specifically in one of seven areas: productivity, relationships, finances, organization, spirituality/ mental well-being, health/ physical fitness and leisure.

(In my book *Habit Stacking (1)*: 97 Small Life Changes That Take Five Minutes or Less, I included 97 small changes you can make in those seven major areas of life and start reaping rewards immediately. All of these things are broken down into specific, actionable routines.)

Element #4: It's simple to complete

Since each habit takes less than five minutes to complete, it's natural that none of the habits are complicated or rigorous. The simplicity of each habit allows you to complete it and move on to the next, sticking to the routine and making a lot of positive changes quickly and efficiently.

Each habit takes only a few small steps to complete. One example is unsubscribing from a retail email newsletter. You can do this by taking a few simple actions that take only a few seconds each.

Element #5: It takes less than 30 minutes

Your complete habit stacking routine should take up just 15 to 30 minutes when you string all of the quick actions together. If you're new to habit stacking, start by focusing on habits that add up to around 15 minutes of your day. This will help you avoid being overwhelmed and ensure you complete all of your habits.

With a 15-minute routine, it's possible for you to complete anywhere from three to thirty small changes. Even if you add new habits, it's important to keep your routine to less than 30 minutes. If you create a routine lasting longer than 30 minutes, there's a chance it will take too much of your time, making it difficult to complete your list.

Element #6: It Follows a logical process

Your habit stacking routine should flow like a well-oiled machine. You complete each action, moving from room to room quickly and consistently. If you take breaks in between actions, you are wasting both time and energy. This could prevent you completing the entire routine.

The whole process should be like a production line, with constant action until all the habits are complete. Every time you complete the routine, it will get easier and become more habitual, resulting in many positive life changes over the course of the next few weeks or months.

Element #7: It follows a checklist

Habit stacking isn't meant to be a guessing game, or to be improvised on a day-to-day basis. It should be a set of actions done the same way, in the same order, each day. The best way to make sure this happens is to have the habits written down in a checklist. That way, you always know which task comes next and feel a sense of accomplishment as you get through each item on your list.

Checklists do much more than keep people organized; they also increase productivity. *The Checklist Manifesto* by Atul Gawande (2) is a great read about how checklists can improve personal productivity. It offers great insight and inspiration for your own habit stacking checklist.

Element #8: It fits your life

It's important to leverage your day in habit stacking. Take advantage of your location and the time of day when it comes to your habits. Energy is usually at its peak during the first part of your day, which means you should be completing habits that inspire or excite you about the day ahead.

A great example is sending an inspirational quote or story to a loved one. It takes energy to find such a piece of content and decide who to send it to, but this habit is highly rewarding and will help you kick off your day feeling great and ready to tackle all the following habits you have in your routine.

Over to You

There you have it— all the important elements of habit stacking. You must take all these elements into account when creating your habit-stacking routine because they all work together to ignite positive life changes.

Because all of the elements work together, you need to include them all in a productive and successful habit-stacking routine.

The right structure of a habit-stacking routine is the foundation for constructive, valuable habits that result in positive changes.

Steve S.J. Scott - based on: *Habit Stacking*: 97 Small Life Changes That Take Five Minutes or Less (1)

Afterword - Where I Got My Ideas From

You may be wondering where I got my ideas from. I've actually had people and early readers of my posts and this book ask me things like:

'Joanna, you're going against the accepted wisdom of habit formation.'

'Are you sure it really works?'

Or even:

'Show me the evidence.'

Yes, it's not a mainstream approach to habit formation, but it works. And if you want to see the evidence - here it is:

Below is the list of the steps (numbers) from my HYH framework and the sources of inspiration.

1-3. What's Your Problem, What Do You Want to Achieve, and Is This Realistic?

I've borrowed the concept of the Desired Outcome and limitations/constraints exploration from **User Experience/User Interface** literature. I was absolutely amazed at how UX/UI folk talk openly about making it all as easy as possible for people to do things they want them to do, removing barriers, following the path of least resistance, etc. And obviously, it's all well backed up with evidence how people think and act. That's why well-designed interfaces work like a dream.

My main sources of inspiration were:

Joe Natoli: *Think First. My No-Nonsense Approach to Creating Successful Products, Powerful User Experiences and Very Happy Customers* (1).

Joe Natoli: *10 Commandments of UI Design* (2).

And many other articles and posts and videos from UX/UI field.

4-6. The Habit Loop

The concept of the habit loop is mainstream. I first learnt about it from the excellent book by Charles Duhigg: *The Power of Habit: Why We Do What We Do in Life and Business* (3).

7-8. Habit Loop 'Hacks'

My habit loop hacks come from many years of trial and error and my discovery of Behavioral Economics and their concept of 'nudging' people towards the 'right choice.'

Although it still raises some ethical dilemmas (and I get it.), there is plenty of evidence that nudging works (4, 5, 6).

Other resources I've used for inspiration:

Kim Ly et al: *The Practitioner's Guide to Nudging* (7)

Susan Weinschenk: *How to Get People to Do Stuff* (8)

Susan Weinschenk: *100 Things Every Designer Needs to Know About* (9)

7-9 Outsmarting Motivation, Willpower, and Other Self-Control Stuff:

As you will certainly discover reading this book, I've got rather unimpressive willpower and my ability to delay gratification is embarrassing. I'm aware that it hinders my progress towards my personal and professional goals. This is why a while ago I embarked on a journey towards improving these aspects of my character and I've been learning a lot about it.

My main sources of inspiration, which are quoted throughout the book, alongside many studies, are listed in the reference section. These books have improved my understanding of how motivation, willpower, and self-control work, and informed my 'outsmart your willpower' approach to habit formation.

References and Further Reading

Introduction:

1. Koch, R. (2004). *Living the 80/20 way*. London: Nicholas Brealey.
2. Wood, W. and Neal, D. (2007). A new look at habits and the habit-goal interface. *Psychological Review*, 114(4), pp.843-863. Accessed at: https://dornsife.usc.edu/assets/sites/545/docs/Wendy_Wood_Research_Articles/Habits/wood.neal.2007psychrev_a_new_look_at_habits_and_the_interface_between_habits_and_goals.pdf
3. Tugend, A. (2010, Oct 09). Pumping Out the Self Control In the Age of Temptation. *The New York Times*; Accessed at: http://www.nytimes.com/2010/10/09/your-money/09shortcuts.html?_r=0

Chapter 1: Why Focus on Habits?

1. Society for Personality and Social Psychology. (2014, August 8). How We Form Habits, Change Existing Ones. *ScienceDaily*.Accessed June 4, 2016 at www.sciencedaily.com/releases/2014/08/140808111931.htm
2. Neal, D.T., Wood, W., Quinn J.M. (2006). Habits - A Repeat Performance. *Current Directions in Psychological Science*, vol.15 no. 4; p: 198-202;Accessed at: https://dornsife.usc.edu/assets/sites/208/docs/Neal.Wood.Quinn.2006.pdf
3. Duhigg, C. (2012). *The power of habit*. New York: Random House. Kindle Edition

Chapter 2: How Habits Work

1. Duhigg, C. (2012). *The power of habit*. New York: Random House. Kindle Edition
2. Beeler, J., Cools, R., Luciana, M., Ostlund, S. and Petzinger, G. (2014). A kinder, gentler dopamine… highlighting dopamine's role in behavioral flexibility. *Front. Neurosci.*, 8. http://doi.org/10.3389/fnins.2014.00004 Accessed at: http://www.ncbi.nlm.nih.gov/pmc/articles/PMC3901300/
3. Wikipedia. (2016). *Reward system*. [online] Available at: https://en.wikipedia.org/wiki/Reward_system [Accessed 6 Oct. 2016].

4. Wikipedia. (2016). *Reward management.* [online] Available at: https://en.wikipedia.org/wiki/Reward_management [Accessed 6 Oct. 2016].

5. McGonigal, K. (2012). *The willpower instinct.* New York: Avery.

6. Lally, P., van Jaarsveld, C., Potts, H. and Wardle, J. (2009). How are habits formed: Modelling habit formation in the real world. *European Journal of Social Psychology*, 40(6), pp.998-1009. Accessed at: http://repositorio.ispa.pt/bitstream/10400.12/3364/1/IJSP_998-1009.pdf

Chapter 3: Why Motivation is Not the Answer to Successful Habit Building

1. Arnett, G. (2015). *How long do people keep their New Year Resolutions?*. [online] the Guardian. Available at: http://www.theguardian.com/news/datablog/2015/dec/31/how-long-do-people-keep-their-new-year-resolutions [Accessed 6 Oct. 2016].

2. Navarro, J et al. (2013), *Fluctuations in Work Motivation: Tasks Do Not Matter.* Nonlinear Dynamics. Psychology and Life Sciences, vol. 17(1):3-22; Accessed at: http://www.ncbi.nlm.nih.gov/pubmed/23244747

Chapter 4: Habits, Willpower, and Self-Control

1. McGonigal, K. (2012). *The willpower instinct.* New York: Avery.

2. Baumeister, R. and Tierney, J. (2011). *Willpower.* New York: Penguin Press.

3. Baumeister, R., Bratslavsky, E., Muraven, M. and Tice, D. (1998). Ego depletion: Is the active self a limited resource?. *Journal of Personality and Social Psychology*, 74(5), pp.1252-1265. Accessed at: https://faculty.washington.edu/jdb/345/345%20Articles/Baumeister%20et%20al.%20(1998).pdf

4. Tugend, A. (2010, Oct 09). Pumping Out the Self Control In the Age of Temptation. *The New York Times*; Accessed at: http://www.nytimes.com/2010/10/09/your-money/09shortcuts.html?_r=0

5. Carter, E., Kofler, L., Forster, D. and McCullough, M. (2015). A series of meta-analytic tests of the depletion effect: Self-control does not seem to rely on a limited resource. *Journal of Experimental Psychology: General*, 144(4), pp.796-815.

Chapter 5: The Secret Power of Systems on Autopilot

1. Kawamoto, K. et al. (2005), *Improving Clinical Practice Using Clinical Decision Support Systems: A Systematic Review of Trials to Identify Features Critical to Success.* British Medical Journal, 330:765 doi: http://dx.doi.org/10.1136/bmj.38398.500764.8F; Accessed at: http://www.bmj.com/content/330/7494/765.short

2. Garg, A.X., et al. (2005), Effects of Computerized Clinical Decision Support Systems on Practitioner Performance and Patient Outcomes: A Systematic Review. *JAMA*. 293(10):1223-1238. doi:10.1001/jama.293.10.1223.Accessed at: http://jama.jamanetwork.com/article.aspx?articleid=200503

3. Latorella, K.A. and Prabhu P.V.. (2000), A Review of Human Error in Aviation Maintenance and Inspection. *International Journal of Industrial Ergonomics* Vol.26 (2), pp.133–161; Accessed at: http://www.sciencedirect.com/science/article/pii/002073738990014X

4. Subrahmanyam, M.; and Mohan, S. (2013). Safety Features in Anaesthesia Machine. *Indian Journal of Anaesthesia*, 57(5), 472–480. http://doi.org/10.4103/0019-5049.120143; Accessed at: http://www.ncbi.nlm.nih.gov/pmc/articles/PMC3821264/

5. Wikipedia. (2016). *Dead man's switch*. [online] Available at: https://en.wikipedia.org/wiki/Dead_man%27s_switch [Accessed 6 Oct. 2016].

Chapter 7: Identify Your Habit Problem

1. Spradlin, D. (2012), HBR: *Are You Solving the Right Problem?* Harvard Business Review; September; Accessed at: https://hbr.org/2012/09/are-you-solving-the-right-problem

Chapter 8: Choose a Habit Goal to Work on:

1. Jast, J. (2016). *Marshmallow Experiment part 1*. [online] YouTube. Available at: https://youtu.be/HO-DNSX5i74 [Accessed 6 Oct. 2016].

2. (2016). *Stanford marshmallow experiment* [online] Wikipedia. Available at: https://en.wikipedia.org/wiki/Stanford_marshmallow_experiment

Chapter 10: Know Your Context

1. Wood, W.; Tam, L.; and Witt, M.G. (2005), Changing Circumstances, Disrupting Habits. *Journal of Personality and Social Psychology*, 88, no 6 p.918

2. Natoli, J. (2015), *Think First. My No-Nonsense Approach to Creating Successful Products, Powerful User Experiences and Very Happy Customers*. Kindle Edition

3. Natoli, J. (n/d) *10 Commandments of UI Design;* Accessed at: http://www.givegoodux.com/training/

Chapter 11: Know Yourself

1. Duhigg, C. (2012). *The power of habit*. New York: Random House. Kindle Edition

2. S.J. Scott. (2014). *Habit Stacking. 97 Small Life Changes That Take 5 Minutes or Less.* Kindle Edition

3. *Zeigarnic Effect.* http://www.psychwiki.com/wiki/Zeigarnik_Effect

Chapter 13: Pick a Cue

1. Wood, W. and Neal, D. (2007). A new look at habits and the habit-goal interface. *Psychological Review,* 114(4), pp.843-863. Accessed at: https://dornsife.usc.edu/assets/sites/545/docs/Wendy_Wood_Research_Articles/Habits/wood.neal.2007psychrev_a_new_look_at_habits_and_the_interface_between_habits_and_goals.pdf

2. Duhigg, C. (2012). *The power of habit.* New York: Random House. Kindle Edition

3. *Amygdala Hijack* Accessed at: https://en.wikipedia.org/wiki/Amygdala_hijack

Chapter 14: Map Out Your Routine

1. *Cognitive Load,* Accessed at: https://en.wikipedia.org/wiki/Cognitive_load#Effects_of_heavy_cognitive_load

2. Berenholtz, S.M. et al.(2004), Eliminating Catheter-Related Bloodstream Infections In the Intensive Care Unit. *Critical Care Medicine,* vol.32(10):2014-20. Accessed at: http://www.ncbi.nlm.nih.gov/pubmed/15483409

3. Arriaga, A.; et al. (2013), Simulation-Based Trial of Surgical-Crisis Checklists. *NEJM* 368:246-253. Accessed at: http://www.nejm.org/doi/full/10.1056/NEJMsa1204720#t=abstract

Chapter 15: Choose Your Reward

1. Deci, E.L. Koestner, R. Ryan, R.M. (1999), A Meta-Analytic Review of Experiments Examining the Effects of Extrinsic Rewards on Intrinsic Motivation. *Psychological Bulletin,* vol. 125(6):627-68; discussion 692-700. Accessed at: http://www.ncbi.nlm.nih.gov/pubmed/10589297

2. *Overjustification Efect.* Accessed at: https://en.wikipedia.org/wiki/Overjustification_effect

3. Weinshenk, S. (2011), *100 Things Every Designer Needs to Know About People.*

4. Milkman, K.L. et al. (2013), Holding the Hunger Games Hostage at the Gym: An Evaluation of Temptation Bundling. *Management Science, Articles in Advance,* pp. 1–17; http://dx.doi.org/10.1287/mnsc.2013.1784 Accessed at: http://opim.wharton.upenn.edu/~kmilkman/2013_Mgmt_Sci.pdf

5. Kirsch P et al. (2003), Anticipation of Reward in a nonaversive differential conditioning paradigm and the brain reward system: an event-related fMRI study. *NeuroImage*, vol.20, issue 2, pp. 1086-1095; Accessed at: http://www.sciencedirect.com/science/article/pii/S1053811903003811.

Chapter 16: Put Your Habit Loop and Habit Plan Together

1. Gollwitzer, P.M. and Sheeran, P. (2006), Implementation Intentions and Goal Achievement: A Meta-Analysis of Effects and Processes. *Advances in Experimental Social Psychology*, Vol.38, Pages 69–119. Accessed at: http://www.sciencedirect.com/science/article/pii/S0065260106380021

2. Webb, T. L.; Sheeran, P. (2006), Does Changing Behavioral Intentions Engender Behavior Change? A Meta-Analysis of the Experimental Evidence. *Psychological Bulletin*, Vol 132(2), pp. 249-268. http://dx.doi.org/10.1037/0033-2909.132.2.249; Accessed at: http://psycnet.apa.org/psycinfo/2006-03023-004

3. *Implementation Intention*. Accessed at: https://en.wikipedia.org/wiki/Implementation_intention

4. Lally, P., van Jaarsveld, C., Potts, H. and Wardle, J. (2009). How are habits formed: Modelling habit formation in the real world. *European Journal of Social Psychology*, 40(6), pp.998-1009. Accessed at: http://repositorio.ispa.pt/bitstream/10400.12/3364/1/IJSP_998-1009.pdf

5. Yin, H.H.; Knowlton, B.J. (2006), The Role of Basal Ganglia in Habit Formation, *Mature Reviews Neuroscience* 7, no 6: 464-476 Accessed at: http://www.nature.com/nrn/journal/v7/n6/abs/nrn1919.html

6. Guise, S. (2013), *Mini Habits: Smaller Habits, Bigger Results*.

Chapter 17: How to Break an Old Habit

1. *Horror vacui (physics)*. Accessed at: https://en.wikipedia.org/wiki/Horror_vacui_(physics)

2. Clear, J. (n/d), *How to Break a Bad Habit and Replace It With a Good One*.Accessed at: http://jamesclear.com/how-to-break-a-bad-habit

3. Duhigg, C. (2012). *The power of habit*. New York: Random House. Kindle Edition

Chapter 18: 5 Strategies to Help You Kick Temptations

1. McGonigal, K. (2012). *The willpower instinct*. New York: Avery.

2. *Dunning-Kreuger Effect*. Accessed at: https://en.wikipedia.org/wiki/Dunning%E2%80%93Kruger_effect

3. *Empathy Gap.* Accessed at: https://en.wikipedia.org/wiki/Empathy_gap
4. Baumeister, R.F. and Tierney, J. (2012). *Willpower: Rediscovering the Greatest Human Strength.* Penguin Press
5. Urban, T. (2016). *Inside the Mind of a Master Procrastinator.* TEDTalk; accessed at: https://www.ted.com/talks/tim_urban_inside_the_mind_of_a_master_procrastinator
6. Jast, J. (2016), *Marshmallow experiment - Part 1.* Accessed at: https://www.youtube.com/watch?v=HO-DNSX5i74
7. Markman, A. (2009). *If You Want to Succeed, Don't Tell Anyone.* Accessed at: https://www.psychologytoday.com/blog/ulterior-motives/200905/if-you-want-succeed-don-t-tell-anyone
8. Gollwitzer, P. M.; et al. (2009). When Intentions go Public. Does Social Reality Widen the Intention-Behaviour Gap? *Psychological Sciences*, vol. 20 (5); Accessed at: http://www.psych.nyu.edu/gollwitzer/09_Gollwitzer_Sheeran_Seifert_Michalski_When_Intentions_.pdf
9. *Loss Aversion.* Accessed at: https://en.wikipedia.org/wiki/Loss_aversion
10. Kahneman, D.; and Tversky, A. (1984). Choices, Values, and Frames (pdf). *American Psychologist.* **39** (4): 341–350. doi:10.1037/0003-066x.39.4.341.; Accessed at: http://psycnet.apa.org/journals/amp/39/4/341/
11. Scott, S.J., (2014), *Bad Habits No More. 25 Steps to Break Any Bad Habit*; Kindle Edition
12. Lally, P., van Jaarsveld, C., Potts, H. and Wardle, J. (2009). How are habits formed: Modelling habit formation in the real world. *European Journal of Social Psychology*, 40(6), pp.998-1009. Accessed at: http://repositorio.ispa.pt/bitstream/10400.12/3364/1/IJSP_998-1009.pdf

Chapter 19: 5 Ways to Kill Resistance Up Front

1. Pressfield, S. (2011), *The War of Art. Break Through the Blocks and Win Your Inner Creative Battles*, Kindle Edition
2. Pressfield, S. (2012), *Turning Pro. Tap Your Inner Power and Create Your Life's Work.* Kindle Edition
3. Thaler, R.H. and Sunstein, C.R. (n/d), *The Illusion of Progress.* Accessed at: https://nudges.wordpress.com/the-illusion-of-progress/
4. Kivetz, R.; Urminsky, O.; and Znehg, Y. (2006), The Goal-Gradient Hypothesis Resurrected: Purchase Acceleration, Illusionary Goal Progress, and Customer Retention. *Journal of Marketing Research*, vol. XLIII, 39-58; Accessed at: http://home.uchicago.edu/ourminsky/Goal-Gradient_Illusionary_Goal_Progress.pdf

5. Heath, C. H. and Heath, D. (2010), *Switch: How to Change Things When Change is Hard*. Kindle Edition

6. *Principle of Least Effort*. Accessed at: https://en.wikipedia.org/wiki/Principle_of_least_effort

7. Choi, J. et al. (2001/2005), *Saving for Retirement on the Path of Least Resistance*. Originally prepared for Tax Policy and the Economy 2001; Accessed at: http://scholar.harvard.edu/files/laibson/files/saving_for_retirement_on_the_path_of_least_resistance.pdf?m=1360041280

8. Shah, A.K. and Oppenheimer, D.M. (2009), The Path of Least Resistance: Using Easy-to-Access Information. *Current Directions in Psychological Science*, vol. 18 no. 4 232-236. Accessed at: http://cdp.sagepub.com/content/18/4/232.abstract

9. *Choice Architecture*. Accessed at: https://en.wikipedia.org/wiki/Choice_architecture

10. Smith, N.S., Goldstein, D.G. and Johnson, E.J. (2013). Choice Without Awareness: Ethical and Policy Implications of Defaults. *Journal of Public Policy & Marketing*: Vol. 32, No. 2, pp. 159-172. Accessed at: http://journals.ama.org/doi/abs/10.1509/jppm.10.114

11. Johnson, E.J. and Goldstein, D.G. (2013), Do Defaults Save Lives? *Science*, Vol. 302, pp. 1338-1339, 2003; Accessed at: http://papers.ssrn.com/sol3/papers.cfm?abstract_id=1324774

12. Hanks, A.S. et al. (2012), Healthy Convenience: Nudging Students Toward Healthier Choices in the Lunchroom. *Journal of Public Health* vol. 34 (3):370-376. doi: 10.1093/pubmed/fds003l; Accessed at: http://jpubhealth.oxfordjournals.org/content/early/2012/01/31/pubmed.fds003.short

13. Guise, S. (2013), *Mini Habits: Smaller Habits, Bigger Results, Big Rewards*. Kindle Edition

Chapter 20: Mini-Habits Strategy for Personal Development

1. DeAngeles T. (2003), Why we Overestimate Our Competence. *American Psychological Association Monitor on Psychology*, vol. 34, No 2. Accessed at: http://www.apa.org/monitor/feb03/overestimate.aspx

2. Wing, R.R and Phelan, S. (2005). Long-term Weight Loss Maintenance, *The American Journal of Clinical Nutrition*, vol. 82 no. 1; accessed at: http://ajcn.nutrition.org/content/82/1/222S.long

3. Dingfelder S.F. (2004), Solutions to Resolution Dilution. *American Psychological Association Monitor on Psychology*, Vol 35, No. 1; Accessed at: http://www.apa.org/monitor/jan04/solutions.aspx

4. Guise, S. (n/d), *The One Push-up Challenge*, Accessed at: http://stephenguise.com/take-the-one-push-up-challenge/

5. Guise, S. (n/d), *Why Mini-Habits is the Greatest Personal Development Strategy Ever*; Accessed at: http://stephenguise.com/why-mini-habits-is-the-greatest-personal-development-strategy-ever
6. Guise, S. (2013), *Mini Habits. Smaller Habits. Bigger Results.* Kindle Edition

Chapter 21: Test, Track, Tweak, and Celebrate Your Progress

1. Clear, J. (n/d), *How to Stick With Good Habits Every Day by Using the 'Paper Clip Strategy'*. Accessed at: http://jamesclear.com/paper-clips
2. Clear, J. (n/d), *How to Stop Procrastinating on Your Goals by Using the 'Seinfeld Strategy'*. Accessed at: http://jamesclear.com/stop-procrastinating-seinfeld-strategy
3. Wansink, B. (2010). *Mindless Eating. Why We Eat More Than We Think.* Bantam. Reprint Edition

Chapter 22: 6 Steps to Discover What Motivates You

1. *Hierarchy of Needs.* Accessed at: https://en.wikipedia.org/wiki/Maslow%27s_hierarchy_of_needs
2. *Self-Determination Theory.* Accessed at: https://en.wikipedia.org/wiki/Self-determination_theory
3. Bénabou, R. and Tirole, J. (2003), Intrinsic and Extrinsic Motivation. *Review of Economic Studies*, vol. 70 (3): 489-520 doi:10.1111/1467-937X.00253; Accessed at: http://restud.oxfordjournals.org/content/70/3/489.abstract
4. Deci, E. L., & Ryan, R. M. (n/d), *Self-Determination Theory - Theory Overview.* http://selfdeterminationtheory.org/theory/
5. Pink, D. H. (2009). *Drive: The Surprising Truth About What Motivates Us.* New York, NY: Riverhead Books.
6. Friesen, C. (2016), *5 Learnable Mindsets of Highly Successful People.* Accessed at: http://www.success.com/blog/5-learnable-mindsets-of-highly-successful-people
7. Friesen, C. (2016). *Achieve. Find Out Who You Are, What You Really Want, and How to Make it Happen.* Kindle Edition

Chapter 23: Dealing with Willpower Shortages and Outages

1. Guise, S. (2013), *Mini Habits: Smaller Habits, Bigger Results, Big Rewards.* Kindle Edition
2. Baumeister, R., Bratslavsky, E., Muraven, M. and Tice, D. (1998). Ego depletion: Is the active self a limited resource? *Journal of Personality and Social Psychology*, 74(5), pp.1252-1265. Accessed at: https://faculty.washington.edu/jdb/345/345%20Articles/Baumeister%20et%20al.%20(1998).pdf

3. Carter, E., Kofler, L., Forster, D. and McCullough, M. (2015). A series of meta-analytic tests of the depletion effect: Self-control does not seem to rely on a limited resource. *Journal of Experimental Psychology: General*, 144(4), pp.796-815.

4. Job, V et al. (2013), Beliefs About Willpower Determine the Impact of Glucose on Self-Control. *Proceedings of the National Academy of Sciences*, vol.10;110(37):14837-42; Accessed at: http://www.ncbi.nlm.nih.gov/pubmed/?term=23959900

5. *18 Famous People Who Always Dress The Same* (n/d), Forbes, Accessed at: http://www.forbes.com/pictures/efkk45klli/steve-jobs/

6. Dizik, A. (2015b), *Meet the People with Almost Nothing In Their Closets*. Accessed at: http://www.bbc.com/capital/story/20160725-meet-the-people-with-almost-nothing-in-their-closets

7. Baumeister, R.F. et al. (2006), Self-Regulation and Personality: How Interventions Increase Regulatory Success, and How Depletion Moderates the Effects of Traits on Behavior. *Journal of Personality*, vol. 74(6):1773-801. Accessed at: http://www.ncbi.nlm.nih.gov/pubmed/17083666

8. Baumeister, R. and Tierney, J. (2011). *Willpower*. New York: Penguin Press.

9. McGonigal, K. (2012). *The willpower instinct*. New York: Avery.

10. Gailliot, M.T., Baumeister, R.F. (2007), The Physiology of Willpower: Linking Blood Glucose to Self-Control. *Personality and Social Psychology Review*, vol. 11(4):303-27; Accessed at: http://www.ncbi.nlm.nih.gov/pubmed/18453466

11. Hagger, M. and Chatzisarantis, N. (2012). The Sweet Taste of Success: The Presence of Glucose in the Oral Cavity Moderates the Depletion of Self-Control Resources. *Personality and Social Psychology Bulletin*, 39(1), pp.28-42. Accessed at: http://psp.sagepub.com/content/39/1/28

12. Vadillo, M., Gold, N. and Osman, M. (2016). The Bitter Truth About Sugar and Willpower: The Limited Evidential Value of the Glucose Model of Ego Depletion. *Psychological Science*, 27(9), pp.1207-1214. Accessed at: https://kclpure.kcl.ac.uk/portal/files/52390632/PSCI_15_1916_R4_preprint.pdf

13. Gómez-Pinilla, F. (2008). Brain foods: the effects of nutrients on brain function. *Nature Reviews Neuroscience*, 9(7), pp.568-578. Accessed at: http://www.ncbi.nlm.nih.gov/pmc/articles/PMC2805706/

Chapter 24: 5 Unusual but Effective Strategies to Build Lasting Willpower

1. Meadows, M. (2016), *Supercharge Your Self-Discipline. 30 Practical Ways to Develop Long-Term Self-Discipline, Build Lasting Willpower and Achieve Your Goals* - audio course; Accessed at: http://www.profoundselfimprovement.com/portfolio-items/supercharge-your-self-discipline

Chapter 26: Help, My Support System Isn't Very Supportive.

1. Rye, J., Rye, S., Tessaro, I. and Coffindaffer, J. (2009). Perceived Barriers to Physical Activity According to Stage of Change and Body Mass Index in the West Virginia Wisewoman Population. *Women's Health Issues*, 19(2), pp.126-134. Accessed at: http://www.ncbi.nlm.nih.gov/pubmed/19272563

2. Ashton, L., Hutchesson, M., Rollo, M., Morgan, P., Thompson, D. and Collins, C. (2015). Young adult males' motivators and perceived barriers towards eating healthily and being active: a qualitative study. *Int J Behav Nutr Phys Act*, 12(1). Accessed at: http://www.ncbi.nlm.nih.gov/pubmed/26169503

3. Scott, S.J., (2014), *Bad Habits No More. 25 Steps to Break Any Bad Habit*, Kindle Edition

4. Babauta, L. (2010), *10 Ways to Deal With the Non-Simplifying Others In Your Life*. Accessed at: http://zenhabits.net/non-simplifying-others/

5. Meadows, M. (2015). How to Build Self-Discipline to Exercise. Kindle Edition

Chapter 27: 'What the Hell?' Effect and Getting Back on Track

1. Lally, P., van Jaarsveld, C., Potts, H. and Wardle, J. (2009). How are habits formed: Modelling habit formation in the real world.*European Journal of Social Psychology*, 40(6), pp.998-1009. Accessed at: http://repositorio.ispa.pt/bitstream/10400.12/3364/1/IJSP_998-1009.pdf

2. Polivy, J., Herman, C. P.; Deo, R. (2010), Getting a Bigger Slice of the Pie. Effects On Eating and Emotion in Restrained and Unrestrained Eaters. *Appetite*. vol. 55(3):426-30. doi: 10.1016/j.appet.2010.07.015.Accessed at: http://www.ncbi.nlm.nih.gov/pubmed/20691231

3. That's the Way the Cookie Crumbles: One Reason Dieting Does Not Work. (2010, Sept, 2.) *The Economist;* Accessed at: http://www.economist.com/node/16943703

4. Zemack-Rugar, Y., Corus, C. and Brinberg, D. (2012). The 'Response-to-Failure' Scale: Predicting Behavior Following Initial Self-Control Failure. *Journal of Marketing Research*, Vol. 49, No. 6, pp. 996-1014; doi: http://dx.doi.org/10.1509/jmr.10.0510

5. Selig, M. (2011), *Beware the 'What-the-Hell Effect,' Especially on Holidays.;* Accessed at: https://www.psychologytoday.com/blog/changepower/201111/beware-the-what-the-hell-effect-especially-holidays

6. Scott, S.J. (n/d), *What-the-Hell Effect: The Slippery Slope to NEVER Eliminating a Bad Habit*. Accessed at: http://www.developgoodhabits.com/what-the-hell-effect/

7. Oettingen, G. (2014), *The Problem With Positive Thinking*. New York Times, Oct. 24, Accessed at: http://www.nytimes.com/2014/10/26/opinion/sunday/the-problem-with-positive-thinking.html

8. Clear, J. (n/d), *Avoid the Second Mistake*. Accessed at: http://jamesclear.com/second-mistake

Chapter 28: Focus on a Keystone Habit to Transform Your Life

1. Duhigg, C. (2012). *The power of habit*. New York: Random House. Kindle Edition

2. Clear, J. (n/d), *Keystone Habits*. Accessed at: http://jamesclear.com/keystone-habits

Chapter 29: How to Build a Miracle Morning Routine in 6 Minutes

1. Elrod, H (2014). *How To Transform Your Life in 6 minutes a Day*. Accessed at: https://www.entrepreneur.com/article/238075

2. Elrod, H (n/d), *The (6-minute) Miracle Morning*, accessed at: http://halelrod.com/6-minute-miracle-morning/

3. Elrod, H and Kiyosaki R. (2012). *The Miracle Morning: The Not-So-Obvious Secret Guaranteed to Transform Your Life (Before 8AM)*; Kindle Edition.

Chapter 30: How to Stack Small Habits for A powerful Impact

1. S.J. Scott. (2014). *Habit Stacking. 97 Small Life Changes That Take 5 Minutes or Less*. Kindle Edition

Afterword:

1. Natoli, J. (2015), *Think First. My No-Nonsense Approach to Creating Successful Products, Powerful User Experiences and Very Happy Customers*. Kindle Edition

2. Natoli, J. (n/d), *10 Commandments of UI Design*; accessed at: http://www.givegoodux.com/training/

3. Duhigg, C. (2012). *The power of habit*. New York: Random House. Kindle Edition

4. Bradshaw, D. (2015), How a little nudge can lead to better decisions. *Financial Times*, Nov, 16. Accessed at: http://www.ft.com/intl/cms/s/2/e98e2018-70ca-11e5-ad6d-f4ed76f0900a.html#axzz49W1bvLXW

5. Thaler, R.H. (2009), Opting In vs. Opting Out. *The New York Times*; Sept, 26; Accessed at: http://www.nytimes.com/2009/09/27/business/economy/27view.html?_r=0

6. Asch, D.A., Volpp, K.G. (2014), Use Behavioural Economics to Achieve Wellness Goals, *Harvard Business Review*, Dec 01; Accessed at: https://hbr.org/2014/12/use-behavioral-economics-to-achieve-wellness-goals

7. Kim Ly, et al. (2013), *A Practitioner's Guide to Nudging.* Accessed at: https://www.rotman.utoronto.ca/-/media/Images/Programs-and-Areas/behavioural-economics/GuidetoNudging-Rotman-Mar2013.pdf.

8. Weinschenk, S. (2014), *How to Get People to Do Stuff. Master the Art and Science of Persuasion and Motivation.* Kindle Edition

9. Weinshenk, S. (2011) *100 Things Every Designer Needs to Know About People.* Kindle Edition.

10. Baumeister, R.F. and Tierney, J. (2012). *Willpower: Rediscovering the Greatest Human Strength.* Penguin Press

11. McGonigal, K. (2012). *The willpower instinct.* New York: Avery.

12. Kahneman, D. (2011). *Thinking, Fast and Slow.* Allen Lane

13. Pink, D. H. (2009). *Drive: The Surprising Truth About What Motivates Us.* New York, NY: Riverhead Books.

Are You Ready To Transform Your Life In The Next 30-Days?

Now that you've learned more about Joanna's foolproof 9-steps to finally break your bad habits and start thriving in your life, are you ready to take it to the next level?

Whether you want to take a DIY route or work with Joanna directly, she has a 30-day plan that is right for you.

You'll start reaping rewards from day 1, even if you have no willpower.

This system is temptation- and resistance-proof.

If you're confident you can go it on your own with Joanna's careful guidance, then sign up for her 30-day DIY program. In this actionable, practical, no-fluff, step-by-step guide, you'll receive:

- A new email each day, 5 days a week for four weeks. These messages are specifically designed to suit your personality and fit in with your life Habit System. They will keep you on track, hold you accountable and give you tips for developing your Habit System in the fastest, most effective and efficient way possible.
- Four weekly Q&A calls where she will personally answer any questions you have throughout the week to offer clarity and suggestions to overcoming common problems.

You're just 30 days away from effortlessly improving your health, wealth, and happiness (or whatever else you're seeking),

If you need more accountability and direct guidance, than consider working with Joanna directly. In this program, you'll receive:

- Everything that is included in the DIY program.
- Three, 30-minute consultations with Joanna to help set up your system, troubleshoot and make sure you'll achieve your goal on time.
- One 15-minute follow up/troubleshooting call 30 days after the completion of your program
- A fail-proof accountability system.

If you're ready to get started, go to **www.theshapeshiftersclub.com/work-with-me** to learn more.

Don't let another day go by, sign up today.

You've seen how Joanna's system works, now it's your turn to start changing your life.

About Joanna Jast

Joanna Jast is a writer, entrepreneur and self-appointed human nature expert. She has dreams of one day inventing a direct brain-computer interface so she can just upload/download knowledge and update her behaviour software in seconds. While the appropriate technology is or is not being invented, she works on improving the existing ways of absorbing knowledge and adapting to change.

"I have been on a journey to change careers (from healthcare to education) for a couple of years, trying to expedite the process of acquiring new knowledge and skills, building credibility and track record – with various results, but always learning from my experience."

Originally a medical doctor, Joanna is a mid-life career shifter with nearly 20 years experience in psychiatry and training in psychotherapy and adult education. She puts her knowledge of neuroscience, cognitive psychology and human nature into practice to help others accelerate their learning and personal change.

Her love for productivity, effectiveness and top-notch mental powers combined with her low threshold for boredom resulted in a passion for finding shortcuts and well-proven habit changing strategies that work.

Hack Your Habits is a result of Joanna's life-long experience in overcoming her natural laziness, sweet tooth and poor willpower to establish good habits and succeed in life.

The strategies described in this book helped Joanna complete her medical training with good grades, achieve native-level fluency in two foreign languages, write three non-fiction books, speed up her professional career, improve her level of physical fitness, lose weight, improve relationships with people and even master her emotional responses.

Joanna is juggling a full-time job, her business, writing, family commitments, and continuous learning. In her spare time, she enjoys reading science-fiction novels and indulging in her love of landscape photography.

She is currently on a mission to help people who are tired of padded-out, wishy-washy, heavy on marketing and light on evidence self-help advice accelerate their learning and personal change. If you want access to more practical, actionable and tried and tested advice on speeding up your success in professional and personal life and would like to find out more about her, visit www.theshapeshiftersclub.com.

Joanna is the author of *Laser-Sharp Focus: A No-Fluff Guide to Improved Concentration, Maximised Productivity and Fast-Track to Success* and *Hack Your Habits*.

Joanna Jast's photo on the back cover by Mary Wilson-Lim, http://www.marywilsonlim.com

Also By Joanna Jast

Laser-Sharp Focus: A No-Fluff Guide to Improved Concentration, Maximised Productivity and Fast-Track to Success and Hack Your Habits.

Unhappy with your productivity? Consumed by distractions, interruptions and wandering mind syndrome? Can't focus and concentrate? Tired of ineffective advice on how to improve your focus?

Whether you're a student, freelancer, entrepreneur (or wanna-be preneur), employee or anyone else dreaming of being able to snap into focus and stayed focused for however long you want, or wondering how to improve your productivity - this book is for you.

Discover how to focus, improve your concentration and memory, maximise your productivity and speed up your success with evidence-based strategies and proven tricks

This book is a practical, step-by-step guide on **how to improve your focus and boost your productivity** with a twist - it helps you identify what's not working first, so you can target your specific problems head-on, without wasting time and energy on stuff that's unlikely to work for you. And once **your mental focus** is laser-sharp **your memory will improve** and your **productivity** will soar, too.

Get your copy today on Amazon at
www.amazon.com/dp/B018RI1HSU.

Made in the USA
Lexington, KY
23 December 2016